The Civil War In My South

The
CIVIL WAR
In My
SOUTH CAROLINA LOWCOUNTRY

JAMES L. HARVEY, JR.

XULON PRESS ELITE

Xulon Press Elite
2301 Lucien Way #415
Maitland, FL 32751
407.339.4217
www.xulonpress.com

Exulon
Elite

© 2022 by James L. Harvey, Jr.

All rights reserved solely by the author. The author guarantees all contents are original and do not infringe upon the legal rights of any other person or work. No part of this book may be reproduced in any form without the permission of the author.

Due to the changing nature of the Internet, if there are any web addresses, links, or URLs included in this manuscript, these may have been altered and may no longer be accessible. The views and opinions shared in this book belong solely to the author and do not necessarily reflect those of the publisher. The publisher therefore disclaims responsibility for the views or opinions expressed within the work.

Unless otherwise indicated, Scripture quotations taken from the English Standard Version (ESV). Copyright © 2001 by Crossway, a publishing ministry of Good News Publishers. Used by permission. All rights reserved.

The picture on the front cover shows the site of the author's ancestral home on the Okatie River in Okatie, South Carolina. Courtesy of Wes Cooler, III., Pickens, South Carolina.

Paperback ISBN-13: 978-1-6628-4774-5
Hard Cover ISBN-13: 978-1-6628-4908-4
Ebook ISBN-13: 978-1-6628-4775-2

Dedication

To

My Wife. Charlotte Harvey

My Children. Ann Margaret and Charles McCraw.
Jay and Melody Harvey

My Grandchildren. Tabitha, Jacob, Mary, and Susanna Harvey

Recognition

To my wife, Charlotte Harvey, for her encouragement, support, and great patience during the writing of this book.

To Ellen Rankin Bartholomew, Debbie Belger, Wes Cooler, III, Bob Connelly, Larry DuBose, Pam Godwin, Julius Huguenin, Kathy Langford, Allen Perry, and Lecia Smith for their genealogical expertise, support, and assistance with my research.

Table of Contents

Preface. xiii
Introduction xix
Chapter 1.   Barnwell. Barnwell District 1
Chapter 2.   Walterboro. Colleton District 5
Chapter 3.   Bluffton. St. Luke's Parish 13
Chapter 4.   George Medicus Harvey 19
Chapter 5.   Battle of Pocotaligo 25
Chapter 6.   Battle of Tulifinny 31
Chapter 7.   Battle of Coosawhatchie 43
Chapter 8.   Battle of Honey Hill 51
Chapter 9.   Battle of Bentonville 75
Chapter 10. Hampton's Legion 79
Chapter 11. Killed in Action 87
Chapter 12. John Henry Patrick Belger 91
Chapter 13. Uzziah Rentz 101
Chapter 14. Noah Cleland 115
Chapter 15. Sherman's War on Civilians 117
Chapter 16. Charles Jones Colcock .123
Chapter 17. Robert E. Lee 129
Chapter 18. Traveller 137
Chapter 19. Lee's Coosawhatchie Letters to His Family 143
Chapter 20. First Federal Black Volunteer Regiment 159
Chapter 21. Federal Victory 163

Chapter 22. Lee's Last Battle 169
Chapter 23. Final Engagements of the Confederate
         Lowcountry Troops............................. 187
Chapter 24. The Civil War and Christianity 191
Chapter 25. Murder Most Foul......................... 195
Chapter 26. Trial and Execution 201
Chapter 27. Growing Up with Jim Crow................. 205
Chapter 28. Conclusion............................... 213

Preface

Considering the current separation in our country based on political and social preferences, one might ask why I chose to write a book about the Civil War In South Carolina's Lowcountry. I am a white, conservative, evangelical Christian male. Therefore, about one-half of the people living in America today probably think I am persona non grata. If you provide me and this book an opportunity for consideration, I think you will learn some new information about South Carolina and her most southern Lowcountry.

Many books have been written about the Civil War. Some have been written about the war in South Carolina's Lowcountry, though most were about Charleston. Very little has been written about the war in my South Carolina Lowcountry, and none about my family's involvement.

I have given particular attention to the Civil War in Beaufort, Jasper, Hampton, Barnwell, and Colleton Counties. These are the counties in South Carolina where my ancestors were born. That's where my roots run deep around live oak trees. Those trees are draped with low-hanging Spanish moss beside coastal rivers, creeks, and pluff mud.

The Civil War In My South

I will honor my ancestors, and I will include, as much as possible, an accurate account of how they lived their lives. My writing will also reflect my worldview. I developed that view through a prism of Christianity, family values, and family history.

Four of my Great Grandfathers and other relatives were Confederate veterans who served honorably in South Carolina Regiments. Some of them were severely wounded. Others were killed in action. I honor their memory, and I am proud of them. None of them enslaved people. Like most men who fought for the South, they were poor farmers fighting to defend their homeland.

Forty-one years after the Civil War, a formerly enslaved person murdered my great Grandfather George Medicus Harvey on Ladies Island in Beaufort County. The killer was intoxicated and angry. He had been terminated from his plantation job by my Great Uncle Howard Harvey, the plantation manager. George was seated in a front porch rocking chair when a shotgun blast shattered his head. I will discuss this more in Chapter 25.

While I honor the memory of my ancestors who fought for the Confederacy, I cannot honor one of the leading causes of our nation's most significant conflicts. South Carolina did secede from the Union over states' rights. But those rights included white citizens enslaving Black men, women, and children. It should be noted the great majority of South Carolinians at that time did not enslave anyone. Most of them were poorly educated and worked on small family farms.

I believe the Civil War took place due to politics and economics. There was a total lack of compromise between the North and the South. Abraham Lincoln made it clear he would not go to war to eliminate slavery. He would only go to war to preserve the Union.

However, wealthy enslavers in the South believed that once the war began, emancipation would follow. There were three to four million slaves in America at that time. Most of them were in the South. Their owners feared their release would result at worst in the murder of themselves and their families and, at best, the loss of their money and property.

Many in the North and some in the South felt that slavery was a sin and should be abolished. However, most of America's white population in 1860 did not believe African Americans would ever be equal to whites. This was made clear by how the Federal Army's commanders and soldiers treated African Americans in the North and South before and during the war.

Slavery was not the initial cause of the war, but it was at the center of the crisis for the South. Southern politicians wanted to be elected and re-elected. To do so, they needed support and money from the educated and large plantation owners (known as "planters") who had made their fortunes from rice and cotton. Their wealth was acquired through the work of their slaves. The politicians needed the planters, and the planters needed their slaves. It was the only way to maintain their current wealth.

Also, talk of the South seceding from the Union started much earlier than 1860. As a result of what was known as the Tariff of Abominations, secession had been discussed by southern politicians and planters at least thirty years before the Civil War began. To protect American industry from foreign competition, the United States implemented tariffs in 1816. The initial tariff duties were reasonable, but the Tariff of Abominations enacted in 1828 increased duties by thirty to forty percent on specific raw materials such as cotton and tobacco. The foreign markets, in retaliation, prohibited the purchase of American cotton, which was the chief export and the cornerstone of the southern states' economy.

The South protested vigorously but to no avail. The matter was laid to rest until January 1830. At that time, United States Senators Robert Hayne from South Carolina and Daniel Webster from Massachusetts had a heated debate on the Senate floor. Hayne argued that each state was sovereign and could nullify federal rulings when those rulings infringed on states' rights. He also asserted that secession would be appropriate to ensure state and individual rights. Webster responded that liberty and union were inseparable. He and other unionists believed that people made up the union, not states. Since nullification would lead to secession, the Union had to be maintained to ensure the protection of its citizens.

There was great support for nullification among South Carolina's citizens. One example of that support occurred in my hometown of Coosawhatchie, South Carolina, during a July 4th celebration in 1832. The *Daily National Intelligencer* newspaper in Washington, DC, published the following article in its July 27, 1832 edition.

> *Nullification Desired at Coosawhatchie.*
> *Nullification—enough of it.*

At the Celebration of the late Anniversary at Coosawhatchie, South Carolina, fifty-nine Toasts were drunk, of which no less than twenty-nine were exactly the same.

> *"Nullification, the rightful remedy." Fourteen out of the remaining thirty contained the word Nullification, of which were the following: "Nullification, Disunion, Civil War, anything rather than peaceful submission to unjust taxation."*

"Nullification, the sooner the better." "Nullification, morning, noon, and night." "Georgia Nullification." "Nullification to the backbone."

There were two voices raised against Nullification, as follows: "Nullification, not the rightful remedy." "The spirit of '76—I am sorry to see so much of disunion, and so little of the '76 spirit amongst us."

These toasts were followed by no cheering, whilst every Nullifying toast was greeted with nine cheers.—Fay. Observer [1]

Since there was no resolution and no willingness to compromise, South Carolina adopted an Ordinance of Nullification effective February 1, 1833. The ordinance made it clear if Congress passed any act involving force, it would result in South Carolina's immediate secession from the union.

Twenty-seven years later, South Carolina did secede from the Union. The state's causes for this action may be found in the *South Carolina Declaration of Causes of Secession. December 24, 1860.* [2]

As indicated above, the South was not the only region of the United States where slavery was supported. Many northern industrialists, people in business, and civic leaders also supported the war for political and economic reasons. Slavery in the South brought financial gain to the North by importing rice and cotton. Slavery has been a part of America's history from its beginning. This fact does not lessen the South's responsibility, but the South does not bear this sin alone.

A reviewer of Walter D. Kennedy's 1944 book, *Myths of American Slavery,* stated,

> *Few issues have inspired as much debate, disgust, and dissent as that of slavery. While modern Americans are unanimous in their condemnation of slavery as cruel, unjust, and contrary to our nation's basic creed of individual freedom, it must be acknowledged that, less than 150 years ago, upstanding citizens legally bought and sold other human beings.* [3]

Introduction

George Medicus Harvey was my paternal great-grandfather. He died 41 years before I was born. He was a husband, father, Confederate soldier, farmer, grandfather, and murder victim. While writing this book, I have learned much about his life.

The effect of the war on him and my other ancestors who served, their families, the rest of South Carolina, and the United States was obviously of great significance. The impact continues to this day. I proudly honor the memory and service of my great grandfathers and other family members. All of them were poor Christian farmers. None of them enslaved people, and all of them thought they were doing the right thing at the beginning of the war.

Slavery is a horrendous stain on America's past. While we can't change the past, we can and should learn from it. I believe the South's history and America's history should be reported and taught truthfully and accurately. It should include the good and the bad. That is what I have attempted to do in writing this book.

I did not know my great grandfather, but I knew his son, Milledge Boynton Harvey. Milledge was my grandfather, and he was born in Bluffton, South Carolina, on June 27, 1876. My Grandmother,

Eulalie Cooler Harvey, was born a few miles away in Okatie on November 20, 1879.

Milledge and Eulalie married in 1900. Around 1905, Milledge took a position as a security guard at the Beaufort County Jail, where he worked for Sheriff James McTeer. Soon after, they moved a short distance to Prichardville and started a life of farming. Four of their seven children were born there.

Milledge and Eulalie Harvey [1]

Milledge and Eulalie Harvey. My Grandparents: Milledge and Eulalie Cooler Harvey. Milledge was born in Bluffton, South Carolina on June 27, 1876. Eulalie was born a few miles away in Okatie on November 20, 1879. They were married for sixty-four years and had seven children. This picture was taken beside their house in Tallahassee, Florida, in 1944.

Introduction

Around 1908, Milledge moved the family to Fernandina Beach, Florida. My father, James Leslie Harvey, Sr., was born there in 1909. The Seaboard Air Line Railroad had hired Milledge to be a locomotive engineer. Working with the Railroad was an excellent opportunity. It enabled him to begin a career and better support his family.

By 1927, the Railroad had transferred Milledge to Tallahassee, Florida. The family lived there for 44 years. Milledge retired from Seaboard with 32 years of service. He died in 1964. Eulalie later moved to Jacksonville, where she lived with her youngest daughter, Doris Harvey Redfern, and her family. She died on November 20, 1970.

My father died one month earlier in October. Because of her age and poor physical condition, the family chose not to tell Eulalie she had outlived her second youngest son.

Milledge and Eulalie were married for 64 years. She continued cooking on a wood stove until she moved to Jacksonville. They were the "salt of the earth," and I loved them dearly. In this picture, they were standing beside their house in 1944. I enjoyed the times I spent with my grandparents in Tallahassee very much. In the 1950s, Granddaddy let me use his pocket knife to carve my initials on the wood railing around the front porch while he sat in the swing and watched. I was back on that front porch on September 30, 1964. I waited to join my family and serve as a pallbearer for granddaddy's funeral. My initials were still in the wood, but the swing was empty.

The house my grandparents lived in was on West Gaines Street in Tallahassee. The backyard was next to the railroad. The neighborhood was semi middle class and friendly. I recently read that a vacant lot on that street had sold for one million dollars. The buyer was going to use it to provide parking for adjacent businesses.

The Civil War In My South

As I grew into adulthood, I became very interested in genealogy; but no one was left alive to tell me about the Harveys. Like many people, I never asked my grandparents or parents to tell me our family's history. The only information I could find about my great grandfather was his name.

My father took me somewhere around Beaufort, South Carolina, when I was very young. When he arrived at his destination, he told me, "This is where your great grandfather was murdered." Many years later, I thought this was just a dream. About ten years ago, I asked my wife to accompany me to the Richland County Library in Columbia, South Carolina. I had read about the Family Research Center located there. After telling the librarian about my dream, she entered some information into her computer. Within minutes, she had found and printed an article published in the *Beaufort Gazette* (Beaufort, SC) newspaper dated August 30, 1906. My dream became a reality, and my days of serious research had begun. [2]

You will read names such as Coosawhatchie, Pocotaligo, Yemassee, Edisto, and others that might be foreign to you. They are all towns in the Lowcountry of South Carolina.

The first inhabitants of those towns were Native Americans belonging to the Yemassee Nation and the Muskogean Language family. *SCIWAY.net* provides the following information:

> *They resided near the mouth of the Savannah River in Beaufort and Jasper counties. A 1707 state act defined the boundaries of the "Yamosee Settlement" as being the area from the Combahee River on the north to the Coosaw, Port Royal (now the Broad River) and Savannah Rivers on the south (The Statutes at Large of South Carolina: Acts from*

> 1682 to 1716, p. 641). Altamaha Town, along the Okatie River, was the principal settlement.
>
> Their population is estimated to have been 2,000 in 1650 and 1,215 in 1715. The Spanish Governor of Georgia had offended them for two years. As a result, they decided to move to South Carolina. Upon their arrival, they were given land at the mouth of the Savannah River. Later, eighty-seven warriors fought with the colonists in the Tuscarora War of 1712. Angered by unfair trade practices, slavery, the whipping of Indians, and encroachment on their land, the Yemassee and several other tribes rose against the British and killed approximately 100 settlers in 1715. After being defeated by Governor Craven, they fled to Florida. That uprising became known as the Yemassee War. [3]

I consider myself a native of Coosawhatchie. I was born in Ridgeland (originally named Gopher Hill), nine miles south of Coosawhatchie, in 1947. Now a small village, she still has some "salt of the earth" folks. And she still has some Bible-believing churches preaching the Gospel.

Some professional historians and authors in South Carolina have done an excellent job recording the Lowcountry's history. Most have focused on Charleston and Savannah. My home and the homes of my ancestors have been mostly overlooked and ignored by modern, national historians and journalists. I understand why. Union Major General William Tecumseh Sherman burned everything to the ground in 1865. The town never fully recovered. The village consisted of service stations, motels, small general stores, and churches during my teenage years. When Interstate Highway

95 bypassed Coosawhatchie, most of the remaining small businesses had to close. The same thing happened to many southern small towns on US Highways 17 and 301.

Coosawhatchie and the surrounding area played an important role in South Carolina's political, industrial, agricultural, social, and religious development during the Colonial era. Before the Civil War, the town began as a trading post dealing with the Yemassee, Euhaw, and Coosa Indians. It started to grow in the early 1700s around the Coosawhatchie River bridge.

In the Coosa language, "hatchie" was translated as river. So, the name Coosawhatchie was chosen by the first white settlers for the village. Since then, her name has been mispronounced by almost everyone who did not reside in South Carolina's Lowcountry. The correct pronunciation is koo-suh-HATCH-ee.

During the 1600s and early 1700s, the Coosa tribe was attacked by colonists and the fierce Yuchi tribe. The Colonial authorities also sanctioned the enslavement of Indians at that time. Many of them were sold to plantations in the West Indies.

Volume One of *The History of Beaufort County, South Carolina*, written by Lawrence S. Roland, published in 1996 by the University of South Carolina Press, provides an early history of the town:

> *Coosawhatchie was never surveyed as a town during the colonial period. During the 1740s, an enterprising Swiss merchant from Purrysburg, S.C., Henry DeSaussure, opened a store and lodge home at the bridge's foot. This was also at the head of the navigation of that small stream which winds*

out to Port Royal Sound. He was the founder of one of South Carolina's most prominent families in the revolutionary and antebellum eras.

Coosawhatchie, which was in the geographic center of the Beaufort District, grew into an important crossroad for the southern parishes and eventually became the county seat for fifty- one years following the American Revolution.

Coosawhatchie continued to grow when it became the stopping point on the stagecoach road between Charleston and Savannah. Because of its strategic location, Coosawhatchie was of great importance during the Revolutionary War. General William Moultrie and Colonel Alexander Mcintosh planned to join forces to block the British march to Charlestown. Steven D. Smith, with the S.C. Institute of Archaeology at the University of South Carolina, writes, "...the battle of Cooswahatchie was fought on May 3, 1779. With the continuing stalemate in the north, the British decided to turn to the southern colonies in hopes that loyalists there would support the effort to suppress the revolution. In December 1778, the British entered Georgia and fought a number of battles there. In early 1779, the Americans under General Benjamin Lincoln advanced against Augusta leaving British Major General Augustine Prevost an opening to move against Charleston by crossing the Savannah River. General Moultrie, with two Continental Regiments, awaited him. Moultrie was camped at

> *Tulifiny Hill in present day Jasper County, with Col. John Laurens at Coosawhatchie.* [4]

Laurens crossed the river on May 3, 1779, disobeying his orders. He skirmished with the advancing British, numbering some 2,400 men. He was quickly forced back across the river and back to Tulifinny Hill. After the battle, morale was so low General Moultrie decided to retreat toward Charleston.

J. D. Lewis, writing about the American Revolution in South Carolina, takes a closer look at Lauren's actions. He states,

> *Lt. Col. John Laurens and his men were in position on a slight rise near the bridge at the Coosawhatchie River. They were guarding the road against the expected assault by about 2,400 British soldiers and Loyalists under Brigadier General Augustine Prevost from Savannah. On May 3, 1779, Lt. Col. John Laurens and a 250-man detachment of the North Carolina Light Infantry were on a mission to bring back the Patriot rear guard before the British cut them off. When they encountered the British, Lt. Col. Laurens chose a bad position for his troops. The British fired long-range artillery at the Patriots, who were powerless to do anything. Lt. Col. Laurens was shot in the arm and his horse was killed by artillery fragments.*
>
> *As Lt. Col. John Laurens was sent back for medical attention, he told Capt. Thomas Shubrick to maintain their position. Once Lt. Col. Laurens left though, Capt. Shubrick ordered the Patriots to withdraw. With many of the soldiers also*

wounded, they fell back to the Tullifinny River, about two miles east. He knew that if they had stayed, the entire group would have been captured. In April of 1781, Colonel William Harden was detached by Francis Marion with about 70 or 80 men to operate against Charleston's British South. They captured a post at Red Hill near the present day Saltketcher Bridge on U.S. Highway 17. They then proceeded south to the bridge where they skirmished against British cavalry. On April 14, they pressed south on the route to Pocotaligo, where the British Fort Balfour was located. Harden convinced the occupants that he had enough men to take the fort, and loyalists inside the fort surrendered. Two British officers had also been captured at a nearby tavern a short time before. [5]

After the colonies gained their independence, Coosawhatchie continued to grow.

That growth included The First Baptist Church at Coosawhatchie. It was erected in 1759 and measured 20 feet by 16 feet. The Church later joined the Charles Town Baptist Association, and Rev. James Smart was installed as the first pastor. He served until 1791. It was located on the south side of the Coosawhatchie River on the stagecoach road from Savannah to Charleston (The King's Highway). It was an offspring of the old Euhaw Baptist Church founded in 1686, which is still standing in Grahamville, S.C. [6]

After the Revolutionary War, a larger church structure with more amenities was built on the same site. Confederate States Army Col. James Washington Moore, from Gillisonville, described it,

> *It was a spacious building for the white and colored accommodation: a large front porch with three front doors for the whites, who had the lower portion of the Church for themselves. There were galleries on three sides of the Church for the colored people, and were reached by two back doors, one on either side of the pulpit.* [7]

After the Civil War, Col. Moore became a state senator and General of the South Carolina Militia. He is buried in the Gillisonville Baptist Church Cemetery in Gillisonville.

An old poem referred to the Coosawhatchie church as a "Blue Cathedral." When I was a young boy, I was told by my Grandmother Ethel Belger Wall, a lifelong resident of Coosawhatchie, that the Church included a crystal chandelier imported from France. During the early 1800s, the church members withdrew from the Charles Town Association and joined the Savannah River Association. The South Carolina Baptist Convention was established in Columbia in 1821, and the fourth annual session was held in the Coosawhatchie Church. Reverend Dr. Richard Furman, Furman University's namesake, was the Convention's president at that session. [8]

Coosawhatchie was coming into prominence due to constructing a courthouse and jail. Several well-known attorneys had moved to Coosawhatchie to practice law, including James L. Petigru, Robert Tillinghast, and John A. Inglis.

Shortly after the Revolution, Mr. Derry Gillison, a man of considerable wealth, and his wife chose to move to Coosawhatchie from Massachusetts. They established a tannery and shoe factory. He was an Irish Protestant who was devout and pious. Soon after his arrival, he established an endowment fund for the Coosawhatchie

Baptist Church. He gave instructions that the fund was to be used "...for the preaching of the gospel for the whites and the colored." Gillison gave generously to the newly established churches of the district. In addition to Coosawhatchie, historical records indicate that he provided funds to "...Euhaw, and Gillisonyule(later Gillisonville) Baptist churches". [9]

An endemic disease was spread in Coosawhatchie during the hot and damp summer climate. The citizens grew concerned about being so close to the river. By the mid-1830s, the town was described as "too sickly to occupy." As a result, the courthouse and jail were moved to Gillisonville in 1836.

The historic Euhaw Baptist Church congregation decided to maintain its supportive role. They constituted a new Church in Gillisonville on March 24, 1832, and retained its name as Coosawhatchie Baptist Church.

The South Carolina Baptist Convention met there in December 1845 and unanimously voted to join the recently formed Southern Baptist Convention. Church members continued to worship in the original Coosawhatchie church during the winters until 1860. The name Coosawhatchie Baptist Church would remain until November 19, 1885, when it changed to Gillisonville Baptist Church. It was placed on the National Register of Historic Places in 1971.

After the capture of Hilton Head, Beaufort, and other sea islands by the Federal troops in the fall of 1861, General Robert E. Lee received command of the coastal military department of South Carolina, Georgia, and East Florida. He established his headquarters in Coosawhatchie, where he planned the strategy and defenses to contain the enemy.

Lee ordered the destruction of the "Blue Cathedral" and other adjoining buildings to prevent their use by the Federal troops. He did not want the buildings to be used as a screen by the enemy if they came up the Coosawhatchie River in an attempt to destroy the railroad. Lee was a Christian and likely worshipped in the church. It must have been a difficult decision for him and one he would not have made had it not been necessary.

In her second edition 1962 book, *The Moving Finger of Jasper*, Mrs. Grace Fox Perry ended her section on Coosawhatchie by writing:

> *Beside all, yet aloof from modernity, is the Coosawhatchie stream, its tidal regularity involved with Broad River and the sea. Its narrow, ridging banks have echoed to the footsteps of Indians, traders, colonists; Tories and Revolutionaries, legislative officials, lumbermen and railway employees, Confederates and Federals; impoverished planters, highway builders, gasoline station attendants and tourist court operators. To listeners in time, above the lapping of its tidal waters travel fleeting, processional sounds swift crack of guns, duet of saw and hammers, quick pat-pat of sawmills, slow chug of farm machinery, whistled blast of trains, insistent honk of autos; timbered beat of "piccolos," rumbling of convoys, shouts of peace celebration, and the far-away, pulsating melody of hymns in the night. Perhaps Coosawhatchie is more than a moss- draped, Lowcountry village. It symbolizes a country.* [10]

I have some experience with historical journalism, but I am not a professional historian or journalist. I have written this book for my family, particularly my grandchildren and others interested in Civil War history and genealogy. It is not intended to be an academic treatise. I have also included forty-six images which I think the general interest reader will appreciate.

One final comment. My family and I are Christians. All of our ancestors were Christians. They were, and those of us still alive today, are sinners. We have been saved only by God's grace. I have written this book striving for an accurate historical account. I hope it will be of interest to a broad and diverse audience.

Unless otherwise noted, all of the towns, churches, and rivers mentioned are located in South Carolina.

While writing this book, I used many different sources. I included firsthand accounts and primary sources when available.

My South Carolina Lowcountry is the land of my parents, grandparents, great grandparents, and many other ancestors. My wife and I will be buried there. It will always be my home.

Chapter 1

Barnwell. Barnwell District

―――――⋙○⋘―――――

George Medicus Harvey, 1835 to 1906, was a husband, father, grandfather, farmer, soldier, gentleman, and a victim of murder. He was also my great-grandfather.

He was born in the Miller Swamp area (current towns of Sycamore and Fairfax) of Barnwell District, South Carolina, in October 1835. His parents were William W. and Eleanor Harvey. George had two brothers, William B. and Washington H., and five sisters, Eveline Green, Teresa Eliz Harter, Rebecca Harrison, Nancy Ann Cope, and Isabelle Russell. George M. Harter later became the guardian for George Medicus and Eveline.

The 1850 U.S. Census indicates George was 14 and living with his sister Rebecca and her husband. They were living in the vicinity of Fairfax, SC. [1]

The *South Carolina Encyclopedia* describes how Barnwell was developed,

Originally located on the old Stage Coach Road from Charleston to Augusta, Barnwell was first called Red Hill. Like Barnwell County, the town was named for John Barnwell of Beaufort. The first county courthouse was built in 1800 on five acres given by Benjamin Odom. Subsequent courthouses were built in 1819, 1830, 1848, 1871, and 1879. With several renovations and additions, the 1879 building continued to serve as the Barnwell County Courthouse into the twenty-first century.

The Barnwell County Courthouse and Sun Dial

Courtesy of Melissa Roberts of Barnwell, SC. 2010. Do not use without written consent.

Although important as the district seat of justice, Barnwell grew slowly. By the mid-1820s the village contained just 120 inhabitants. The town was incorporated in December 1829. The line of the South Carolina Canal and Rail Road Company passed some ten miles to the west of Barnwell in the 1830s, and the town's economic importance declined relative to the newer railroad towns such as Blackville and Williston. Barnwell would not gain a railroad until 1880, when a short line connecting the town with Blackville was completed.

Late in the Civil War, in February 1865, Barnwell was occupied by federal troops under the command of General Hugh Judson Kilpatrick. Most businesses and public buildings, except for the churches, were destroyed. As a result, the county courthouse resided for several years in nearby Blackville before returning to Barnwell in 1875. Court was held in the Barnwell Presbyterian Church until a new courthouse was completed in 1879. Despite the carnage wrought by the war, more than a dozen antebellum houses survive in Barnwell, including the office used in the latter half of the 1800s by Dr. Todd, a physician and brother-in-law of Abraham Lincoln.

Perhaps Barnwell's most enduring feature is the 1858 freestanding vertical sundial located in front of the courthouse. It was given to the town by Joseph Duncan Allen, a wealthy planter, politician, and soldier. In 1907 a portion of the five acres given by Benjamin Odom, later containing the Confederate Monument, was named Calhoun Park. [2]

The Civil War In My South

Winton County Court House Site

Inscription: Originally Barnwell County was part of Granville County. Later a part of Orangeburg District, Winton County was created by act of the legislature Mar. 12, 1785. Justices William Robertson, John Parkinson, Thomas Knight, Richard Treadway, Daniel Green, William Buford and James Fair were directed to erect a court house, gaol, pillory, whipping post and stocks. These were built of pine logs. Winton County became Barnwell District in 1798 and Barnwell County in 1858.

Erected by Gen. John Barnwell Chapter D.A.R

Chapter 2

Walterboro. Colleton District

My Great Grandmother, Eleanor Boynton, and her family were well known and respected in Barnwell and Colleton Districts. Her father owned a plantation in Walterboro, where Eleanor was born in December 1834.

She had seven siblings: Thomas Evington Boynton, 1829-1898; Elizabeth Boynton Rowell Crawford, 1832-1906; Martha M. Boynton Bunton, 1836-1903; Stephen C. Boynton, 1837-1862; Moses Marden Boynton, 1841-1890; Cornelius Franklin Boynton, 1848-1904; and Catherine Boynton, 1850-1852, age two.

The old Colleton District has a rich history. According to *old-places.org,*

> *The community now called Walterboro was settled in 1783 by two brothers, Paul and Jacob Walter. Originally from Germany, the Walters had settled in Old Dorchester, but Paul and Jacob later purchased rice plantations near Jacksonborough, called Whitmarsh and Boundary Farm respectively.*

> Paul's daughter, Mary, was 'sickly' and in order to get her into a healthier environment, the brothers went in search of a summer home for their families. They named the place they found "Hickory Valley." Two other Walter brothers, John and Isaac, and other planter families joined them here in the summer months. All the original homes were built of logs, with log chimneys and shingled roofs. Paul Walter built the Bethel Presbyterian Church on what became known as 'Walter Hill.'
>
> A private Academy which also was used for Episcopal Church services, existed in Hickory Valley prior to 1825. On the site where the elementary school now stands was The Old Academy, which was a four room schoolhouse. It was finally moved down the street, across from the old high school, to make room for a larger grammar school. Other private academies were later established in Walterboro, but free schools did not exist until after 1880.
>
> Walterboro became the county seat of the Colleton District in 1817, and in the fall of 1822, the first term of court was held in the new courthouse. The town was officially incorporated in 1826. [1]

Before her marriage, Eleanor wrote a letter on November 11, 1854, to her cousin Mahala Rose Preacher in Liberty County, Texas. A copy of part of the original letter is included in this narrative. In addition to family matters, the letter provides some interesting information relative to the 1854 "Carolina Hurricane."

Walterboro. Colleton District

A complete transcript of the letter follows:

November 11, 1854

Dear Cousin, Your kind loving and long looked for letter came to hand yesterday evening & read instantly. You can't imagine the inexpressable joy it gave me to receive a letter from one so much beloved by me though never seen, and God only knows whether we will ever meet this side of eternity though I hope to the reverse. I hope we all may have the pleasure of greeting each other before we leave this world. It is my constant prayer to God to grant us before we die to have the pleasure of speaking to one another. I would make any creditable sacrifice to meet you all in this world.

Dear Cousin I truly sympathize with you in the death of your darling babe but we all know it is now at rest in Jesus' arms. It is no more expose to the trials of this unfriendly World; no it is freed from all. My dear, mourn not it's loss. It was for it's eternal gain moreover it was Gods will. His will must be done. God has promised to be with us to the end, all we have to do is to give our hearts to him, deny our own selves, take up His cross and follow him. I have been trying to serve my God for the last five years and by his help I will serve him till I die. I can but perish if I go I am resolved to try for if I stay away I know I must forever die. If I perish I will pray and perish only there. I can do nothing without God's help, Help us Oh God I pray.

My dear Cousin, it must have been very distressing when those Citys were destroyed. The storm raged in South Carolina at the time but not so bad as in Texas. Great damage was done in Charleston especially to the Battery it will take $20,000 to repair in the tops of several buildings were blowed off. Sullivians Island (in sight of Charleston) some 12 houses were swept away the ladies and children took refuge to the forts and churches the water was so high on the Island it went in the Churches in got higher and higher till the individuals was compelled to get on the backs of the pews. They were in that condition 48 hours without victuals. The small children were almost starved. The ladies would sit on the pew backs with their babes in their arms and the poor creatures were so over come with sleep till they would nod and let the little ones drop on there arms in the waters. Then the little fellows would scream till they were taken up which would be very quick course. Those that fled to the fort were a little better off with the exceptions of one a lady, she gave birth to a fine heir while in there: some 125 I believe were in the fort at the same time. I feel sorry for her.

Nothing serious occurred to us. Dearest one I am feeling quite lonely now since the folks and all moved to their Winter Seats. Only five families are left in the inland with ours. Those five live here Winter and Summer. Crops are tolerable good in Colleton also in Barnwell Dist - and Beaufort Dist as far as I have heard. I have a brother (Stephen) the same age of Cousin George who weighs 130

Walterboro. Colleton District

pounds, a noble looking youth he is. My eldest Bro is fine looking. He is a clerk in a store in Walterboro. Ma's children's names are as follows: Thomas the eldest, Elizabeth next. Eleanor which is my name. Martha next. Stephen next then Moses Cornelius 5 years old. Ma had children vert fast — Give my love to Cousin Howell, Aunt Grandma and my dear little cousins. Accept my sincerest to yourself. I expect it would ever be out of my power to go to Texas though if I could I would go to you on the wings of Pegasus. I tell you select a beau for me and send him off to Colleton SC. I will be satisfied with him. I will kick my beau home, take him and go to you. [2]

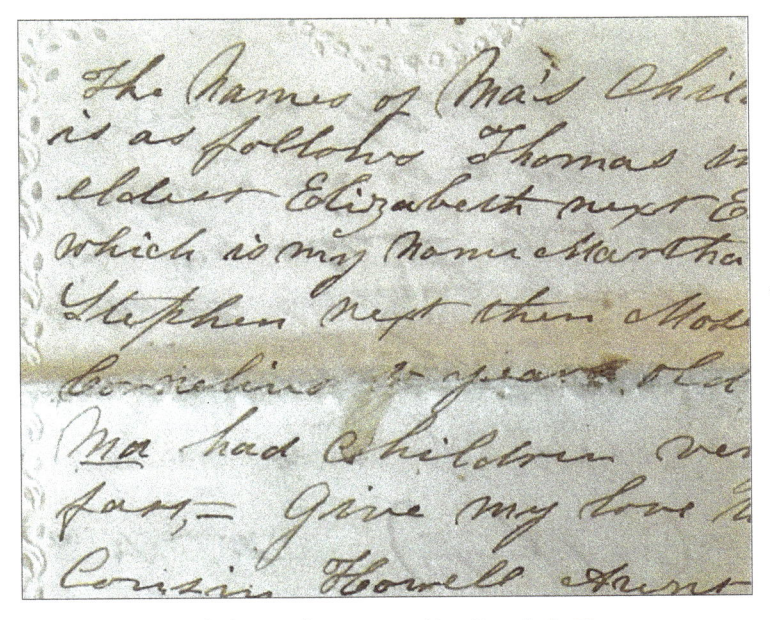

Part of Eleanor's Letter to Her Cousin in Texas.

November 11, 1854

During her teen years and early 20s, Eleanor spent most of her time in Walterboro. After her marriage to George in 1860 they settled in Waterboro, and George took a job as an "Overseer."

Encyclopedia.com states that Antebellum Overseers,

> *were the middlemen of the antebellum South's plantation hierarchy. As such they occupied an impossible position. The masters expected them to produce profitable crops while maintaining a contented workforce of slaves-slaves who had little reason to work hard to improve the efficiency of the plantation. It would have required a prodigy to balance these competing pressures to the complete satisfaction of both the master and the slaves. Few overseers were prodigies.*
>
> *No one knows for sure how many overseers there were in 1860, but the best estimates are that the number of overseers was roughly equal to the number of plantations with thirty or more slaves. These men were a varied lot. Some were the sons of planters who served their fathers as overseers, learning the art of plantation management before striking out on their own. Others, perhaps the largest number, were semiprofessional managers hoping one day to set up their own agricultural operations. And still others lived up to the worst reputation of their class: violent men, often drunkards, unable to hold steady jobs, who moved repeatedly from plantation to plantation. But the average overseer rarely lasted in any master's service for more than a few years. The best moved*

on to other things. The worst were fired. And even the merely competent rarely satisfied an employer for long. [3]

George's work as an overseer in Walterboro might have been for his father-in-law, Moses W. Boynton. From what I have learned about his character, I do not think George would have been a cruel supervisor.

While in Walterboro, George and Eleanor had two children, Ann and Elizabeth.

**Colleton County Court House
Walterboro, South Carolina**

Chapter 3

Bluffton. St. Luke's Parish

Bluffton was initially part of St. Luke's Parish. It was located in what was then Granville County. Lord Cardross, a leader of the Scottish settlement in Beaufort, told the Yemassee Indians they were welcome to live in that part of the Lowcountry. History tells us they established ten towns with a population exceeding 1,200.

After the Indians were taken advantage of for numerous years, the Yemassee War broke out in 1715. Several years of the fighting occurred between the Indians and white settlers. These battles took place from the coast to the Lowcountry parishes' inland areas. The Yemassee tribes were finally defeated when the British army sent reinforcements. They migrated to Florida, thus making the "Indian Lands" available for additional European settlement.

In 1718, the Lords Proprietors established several new baronies. One of them was the Devil's Elbow Barony. The future town of Bluffton would be located there. The first man to have a title to the land was Sir John Colleton, a Barbadian planter. New colonists began building plantations there around 1728. They planted corn, indigo, and cotton.

The Civil War In My South

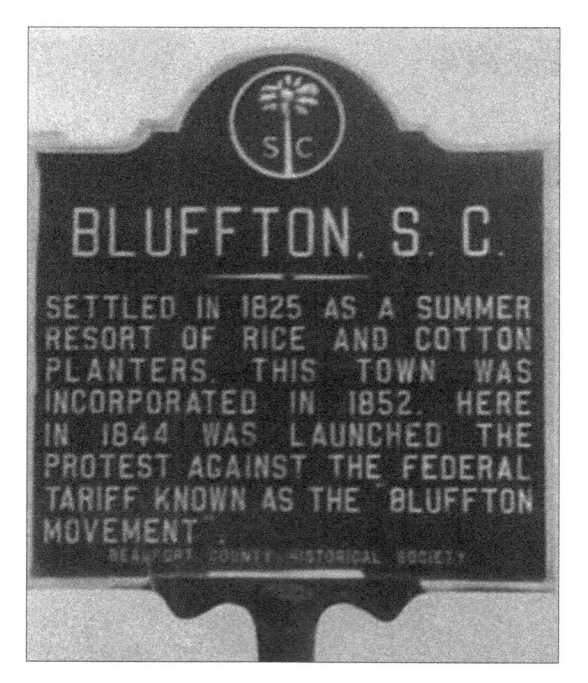

Original Bluffton Historical Marker

**Courtesy of Michael Reynolds
Bluffton, South Carolina**

Before he died in 1776, Sir John Colleton, the original owner's grandson, built plantations near the Victoria Bluff and Foot Point locations. He later sold much of the land to the Rose and Kirk families. The British army, led by General Prevost, burned the plantations three years later.

During the eighteenth century, a large part of the land south of the May River was planted with rice fields. This area is now known as Palmetto Bluff. Rice was a profitable crop for the Lowcountry plantation owners until the early 20th century, when a series of very destructive storms ended rice cultivation.

Bluffton. St. Luke's Parish

Benjamin Walls and James Kirk united two sections of their land to form the town of Bluffton. These plantation owners built the first houses in the early 1800s. "Mill's Atlas" of 1825 referred to the area as "Kirk's Landing" or "Kirk's Bluff." It was not until the 1830s that the first streets were laid out. In the early 1840s, the Kirk and Pope families agreed to name it Bluffton.

George and Eleanor moved from Walterboro to Bluffton in 1860. They bought land and started farming. Bluffton was a nice place to live and rear a family. But, they had moved to what would be known as the birthplace of secession, the "Bluffton Movement." The movement began under what is now known as the Secession Oak. It was led by R. Barnwell Rhett on July 31, 1844.

In the 1850s, a landing for steamboats was constructed, and Bluffton soon became the commercial center of southern Beaufort County. The South Carolina General Assembly incorporated the one square mile town in 1852.

George joined the 3rd South Carolina Cavalry when the Civil War broke out. I have found no record indicating that Eleanor returned to Walterboro with her two daughters to live with her parents. But, I think it is most likely that she did so.

The Bluffton Expedition

After the Union won the Battle of Port Royal on November 7, 1861, Confederate Brigadier General Thomas F Drayton evacuated the Confederate forces from Hilton Head to Bluffton. A large picket headquarters in Bluffton could also monitor the Union's South Atlantic Blockading Squadron operating in the Port Royal Harbor.

In May 1863, the Federal Commander of the Department of the South, Major General David Hunter, ordered that Bluffton be destroyed by fire. His orders were carried out on June 4, 1863. Approximately two-thirds of the town's estimated 60 structures were burned. Two churches and fifteen residences remained after the attack. Today, eight antebellum homes and the two churches still exist in Old Town. That area is now a nationally registered historic district.

For a comprehensive account of the Federal army's destruction of Bluffton, see Jeff Fulgham's *The Bluffton Expedition: The Burning of Bluffton, SC, During the Civil War.* [1]

The Secession Oak

In the early 1950s, my parents and I visited Okatie to see the old house my Grandmother Eulalie Cooler Harvey was born in on November 20, 1879. It was located on the bank of the Okatie River.

After visiting there, Dad drove us to Bluffton, where my Grandfather Milledge Boynton Harvey was born on June 27, 1876. I don't know if Dad ever knew the location of the house where his father grew up, but I have never been able to locate the site. At that time, Bluffton was much like it was many years earlier. The only places I remember seeing from that visit were the Church of the Cross, the adjacent boat landing on the May River, and an old oak tree.

Since that time, the growth of Bluffton, Okatie, Hilton Head, and the surrounding area has been most remarkable. According to "World Population Review," Bluffton was the sixteenth most significant city in South Carolina in 2021, with a population of 30,937. [2]

Bluffton. St. Luke's Parish

The Secession Oak
From *South* Magazine, February 8, 2017

Dad told me the live oak tree was famous. It was years later when I learned this was the Secession Oak. Thought to be around 300 years old, many historians still view it as the birthplace of the "Bluffton Movement," which sparked the state's decision to secede from the Union. It was under this tree in 1844 where radical "fire-eater" Robert Barnwell Rhett, in front of an exuberant crowd, declared it was time to secede.

South Carolina's political forces collided with the general public's poor regard for the federal government. The result led to the state's secession, and the movement would ultimately split the country in half.

Barry Kaufman, writing in *South* magazine in 2017, said,

> *When a group of wealthy planters invited Rhett to speak in the sleepy little farming town of Bluffton, it must have been quite the occasion to draw nearly 500 people (by some accounts) to hear him speak*

in the shade of a twisting live oak tree just off the May River. The contents of his speech are lost to history, but what is known is that his words ignited the crowd and helped launch the term 'The Bluffton Movement' as contemporary shorthand for secessionist sentiment.

Indeed, the term 'The Bluffton Movement' shows up time and again in newspapers and letters from that era right up until Christmas Eve of 1860, when South Carolina seceded from the Union. [3]

Chapter 4

George Medicus Harvey

Great Grandfather George rode his horse from Bluffton to Hardeeville, about 15 miles. When he arrived, he and his horse joined the Confederate Army. The limited funds available to the Confederate army required the soldiers joining the cavalry to provide their mounts. When South Carolina seceded from the Union on December 20, 1860, and fired the first shots at Fort Sumter in Charleston Harbor, the Civil War had begun.

George was enlisted and mustered in for the duration of the war by Captain Young on May 12, 1862. He served in Company F, 3rd South Carolina Cavalry, (St. Peter's Guards) 2nd Regiment.

Captain Henry C. Smart was in command, and company F was first designated as Captain Smart's Company, South Carolina Volunteers. During the war, it would have several name changes and was finally designated Company F, 3rd Regiment, South Carolina Cavalry.

Men joining the Confederate army had choices concerning the length of their enlistment. They could join for the duration of the war, for one year or a lesser time. During General Lee's assignment at Coosawhatchie, this was a constant problem. Many men signed up for one year or less, resulting in a continuing lack of available soldiers to fight in the war. George chose "for the war,' and he served every day until it ended.

My great grandfather's regiment was part of the 8th Battalion, also known as Colcock's Battalion. It was organized in May 1862 by joining seven independent companies of Cavalry. In August 1862, it was increased to a regiment and designated the 3rd Regiment, South Carolina Cavalry.

Many of the men had previously served in the 1st Regiment of the South Carolina Mounted Militia.

Commanded by Col. Charles Jones Colcock, Sr., the Battalion fought in ten battles. Four of them occurred in the Battalion's local area. Pocotaligo, Tulifinny, and Coosawhatchie took place on October 22-23, 1862. The fourth was the Battle of Honey Hill on November 30, 1864. All of these battles resulted in Confederate victories against overwhelming Federal forces. George fought in all of them.

At the beginning of the war in 1861, the Confederate generals ordered silk battle flags for their units. In Richmond, Virginia, the quartermaster bought the entire silk supply for making the flags. Since the only red-like colors available in bulk were either pink or rose, the first battle flags were a lighter shade of pink than the red envisioned by the general staff. According to noted vexillologist Greg Biggs, General P.G.T. Beauregard told the Quartermaster in no uncertain terms, "dye it red sir, dye it with your blood!" [1]

The author is standing beside the original flag of the 3rd Cavalry Battalion, South Carolina Volunteers. Courtesy of the South Carolina Confederate Relic Room & Military Museum, Columbia, South Carolina. October 27, 2021. Photo by Andy Newell, Lexington, South Carolina.

George's "Camp Muster Roll Cards" indicate he was always present for duty, with one exception. The record for November/December 1864 states, "absent, detached to drive cows." [2]

South Carolina 3rd Cavalry Regiment

Officers

Charles J. Colcock, Sr., Col.
Thomas J. Johnson. Lt. Col.
John Jenkins, Major.

Staff

Thomas Hutson Colcock. Lt. Adj.
Thomas Corde. Capt.
T.M. Hutson. Surgeon
N.F. Kirkland. Asst. Surgeon
A.W. Lourey. Capt.
J.G. Williams. Chaplain

Assignments

3rd Military District of South Carolina. Department of South Carolina, Georgia, and Florida. July 1862-July 1864.

2nd Military District of South Carolina, Department of South Carolina, Georgia, and Florida. Company I. March-November, 1863.

1st Military District of South Carolina, Department of South Carolina, Georgia, and Florida. Company K. March-May 1863.

6th Military District of South Carolina. Department of South Carolina, Georgia, and Florida. Company I. December 1883-May 1884.

McLaws' Division. Department of South Carolina, Georgia, and Florida. July 1864-January 1885.

Robertson's Brigade, Department of South Carolina, Georgia, and South Carolina. Company B. November 1864.

Harrison's Command. Taliaferro's Brigade. Department of South Carolina, Georgia, and Florida. Company B. December 1864.

George Medicus Harvey

Jenkin's Command. Taliaferro's Brigade. Department of South Carolina, Georgia, and Florida. Companies I and K. December 1884.

Chesnut's Command. Taliaferro's Brigade. Department of South Carolina, Georgia, and Florida. Companies C and E. December 1884.

Battles

Pocotaligo/Tulifinny/Coosawhatchie. October 22-23, 1862.
Expedition to Bluffton. June 4, 1863.
John's Island. December 28, 1863.
South Newport. August 18, 1864.
Honey Hill. November 30, 1864.
Siege of Savannah. November 12, 1864.
The Carolinas' Campaign. January 1, 1865.
Bentonville. April 26, 1865.

Companies

The roster for the 3rd Cavalry Regiment contains 2,082 names.

Company A. Marion County. Men of Combahee.
Company B. Colleton County. Colleton Rangers.
Company C. Beaufort County. Beaufort District Troop.
Company D. Barnwell County. Barnwell Dragoons.
Company E. Hampton County. Calhoun Mounted Men.
Company F. Barnwell and Hampton Counties. St. Peter's Guards.
Company G. Charleston County. German Hussars.
Company H. Charleston County. Ashley Dragoons.
Company I. Colleton County and Sea Islands. Rebel Troop.
Company K. Barnwell County. Savannah River Guards.

Additional Harveys in Company F.

The following Harvey men also served with my Great Grandfather in Company F, with the 3rd Cavalry. Some are from Coosawhatchie, and likely all of them were relatives.

H.B. Harvey
J.L. Harvey
J.M. Harvey
J.W. Harvey
O.L. Harvey
S.E. Harvey

Source: *Historical Sketch And Roster Of The South Carolina 3rd Cavalry Regiment.* John C. Rigdon. 2018. Page 175. [3]

William B. Harvey

Great Grandfather George's older brother, William B. Harvey, also enlisted in the Confederate States Army (CSA.). He was born in Barnwell District in 1832. When he grew older, he moved to Lake City, Florida. He enlisted there in the CSA on October 3, 1861. On October 6th, he was mustered into Company A, 1st Battalion Cavalry.

William was wounded on May 18, 1864, in Richmond, Virginia. He survived the war and returned to his family in Florida in 1865. He died there on January 3, 1890.

Chapter 5

Battle of Pocotaligo

The Battle of Pocotaligo took place on October 22-23, 1862, in Pocotaligo, Tulifinny, and Coosawhatchie. The Union's objective was to sever the Charleston and Savannah Railroad and thus isolate Charleston, South Carolina.

Great Grandfather George fought in these battles. As mentioned previously, he was a member of Company F, 3rd South Carolina Cavalry. He and his compatriots were dispatched from Grahamville as reinforcements.

Also, one of my maternal 2nd Great Grandfathers, John H.P. Belger, fought in these battles with the 11th South Carolina Infantry Regiment.

Battle of Pocotaligo

Courtesy of *47th Pennsylvania Volunteers: One Civil War Regiment's Story*

On October 21, 1862, the Union's force of 4,200 men, under the command of Brigadier General John M. Brannan, boarded transport ships and left Hilton Head. Brannan's orders were "to destroy the railroad and railroad bridges on the Charleston and Savannah line."

Under the protection of a Naval Squadron, they sailed up the Broad River, disembarking the following day at Mackay Point (between the Coosawhatchie and Pocotaligo Rivers), less than ten miles from the railroad.

The 47th and 55th Pennsylvania Infantry Regiments, under the command of Colonel Tilghman H. Good, began the march toward Pocotaligo. A smaller detachment of 300 men — two companies of engineers and the 48th New York regiment — moved up the Coosawhatchie River with orders to attack the bridge at Coosawhatchie and then turn towards Pocotaligo, tearing up the rails as they went.

Walker called for reinforcements from Charleston and Savannah and deployed his Confederate forces to meet the two Union advances, sending 200 men to guard the bridge. At the same time, the Beaufort Volunteer Artillery (CS), supported by two companies of cavalry and some sharpshooters, was dispatched to meet the main Union advance on the Mackey Point road. Brannan's Division encountered the Rebels near the abandoned Caston's Plantation when the Confederate artillery opened fire with their two howitzers. The Confederates retreated when the Union artillery responded.

Walker slowly withdrew, making a rolling defense while Brannan moved in pursuit, eventually falling back to the defensive works at Pocotaligo. The Union advance stalled when they encountered the Confederates on the opposite side of a muddy marsh. They blazed away at one another for more than two hours with musket and cannon fire until the arrival of Confederate reinforcements.

As night fell, Brannan, realizing that the railroad bridge was out of reach, ordered retreat up the Mackay's Point road to the safety of his flotilla, the 47th Pennsylvania forming the rearguard, with the Rutledge Mounted Rifles and Kirk's Partisan Rangers in pursuit. Brannan's troops re-embarked at Mackay's Point and returned to Hilton Head.

Colonel Edward W. Serrell, First New York Engineers, made this report to his superiors,

War of the Rebellion: Serial 020 Page 0155 Chapter XXVI. SKIRMISH AT COOSAWHATCHIE, S.C., ETC.

Numbers 5. Reports of Colonel Edward W. Serrell, First New York Engineers.

HEADQUARTERS UNITED STATES FORCES,
Broad River, S. C., October 22, 1862

CAPTAIN: I have the honor to report, for the information of the general commanding the forces, that, agreeably to the orders of the major-general commanding the department, I reported to Brigadier-General Brannan this morning at 8 o'clock with 250 enlisted men of the Volunteer Engineers and 15 officers constituting the engineer force. Fifty-four men and two officers were assigned to duty with Colonel Barton, of the Forty-eighth New York Volunteers, and furnished with tools and the proper appliances for destroying railroad structures. This detachment was placed under the orders of Captain Samuel C. Eaton, of the Volunteer Engineers, and has not yet been heard from. The remaining forces of the Engineers were placed under the immediate orders of Lieutenant Colonel James F. Hall, of the Volunteer Engineers. I was assigned to duty on the commanding general's staff.

The line of march was from Mackay's Point, on Broad River, on the direct road toward Old Pocotaligo. The general direction is about north from the Point, and the road is on the right bank of the Pocotaligo River, and begins at the confluence of the Pocotaligo and Broad Rivers, and lies from one to three-quarters of a mile from one to three-quarters of a mile from this stream. The country through which the road runs is a rolling sandy plain, except at two points, where it crosses marshes and small streams, the first of which is about 5 1/2 miles from the Point, and is on Caston's plantation; the second is about 6 1/4 miles, and the plantation is called Frampton.

Battle of Pocotaligo

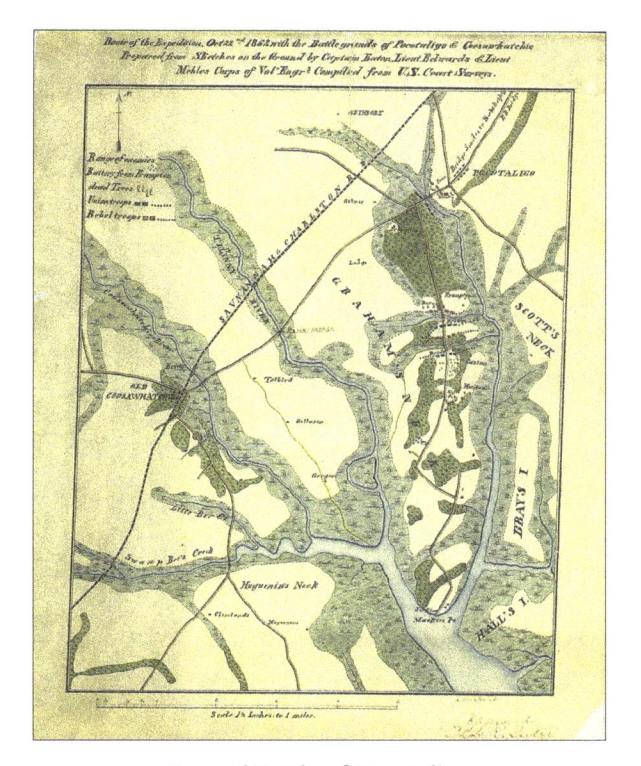

Second Battle of Pocotaligo

Map of the battle and route of the expedition
Wickiwand.com

At both of these points serious engagements took place with the rebels. The Engineer troops were engaged from about 10 o'clock until after sunset in making and repairing several small bridge and keeping the road in order. Lieutenant-Colonel Hall reports Sergt. N. M. Edwards, acting lieutenant, as especially worthy of notice for his efforts in repairing the bridge at Frampton under heavy fire and for his general efficiency.

The point reached by the troops was within a few yards of the road bridge over the Pocotaligo, on the road leading from Old Pocotaligo to Coosawhatchie. This bridge was destroyed by the rebels as they retreated over it into their earthworks on the easterly side. Timber for the purpose of rebuilding this bridge was prepared by the Engineers, and was ready to be put together when the retreat was ordered. This point is within about 1 1/2 miles of the Charleston and Savannah Railroad. Officers in the advance report having seen the cars passing. A small lunette, that had been abandoned, was observed on the southerly side of the marsh on the high ground near Caston's.

I have the honor to be, your most obedient servant,

EDWARD W. SERRELL,

Colonel of Vol. Engineers, and Chief Engineer Dept. of the South.

Captain LOUIS J. LAMBERT.

Asst. Adjt. General, U. S. Forces, Broad River, S. C.

OCTOBER 23, 1862

I cannot too highly compliment Lieutenant-Colonel Hall for his zeal and efficiency in caring for the wounded of the whole army during the night.

Source: The Ohio State University Department of History. [1]

Chapter 6

Battle of Tulifinny

The Battle of Tulifinny, four miles south of Pocotaligo, was one of the United States Marines' first times in combat as infantry. It is worth noting they were soundly defeated by the Confederate forces, which included the entire Corps of Cadets of the South Carolina Military Academy (now The Citadel).

The Citadel's website states,

> *The Citadel is a landmark in Charleston and South Carolina that is noted for its educational reputation as well as its rich history. Founded in 1842, The Citadel has an undergraduate student body of about 2,300 students who make up the South Carolina Corps of Cadets. Another 1,000 students attend The Citadel Graduate College, a civilian evening and online program that offers graduate and professional degrees as well as undergraduate programs.*

The Civil War In My South

> *The Citadel is best known nationally for its Corps of Cadets, which draws students from about 45 states and a dozen countries. The men and women in the Corps live and study under a classical military system that makes leadership and character development an essential part of the educational experience.* [1]

Citadel Cadets who fought at the Battle of Tulifinny

Cadets Isham G. Harrison, Peter K. McCully Sr., and John E. Lewis standing from the left. Seated: Cadet David S. Taylor, left, and an unidentified cadet.

Col. John C. Sellers, from Sellers, South Carolina, wrote a lengthy letter concerning his remembrances at Tulifinny. It provides a first-hand report of the Citadel Cadets' contribution to the Confederacy. It is from The Citadel Archives and Museum. [2]

Capt. Ben S. Williams, Brunson, S.C.- My Dear Sir: I have greatly enjoyed reading your memoirs as published in the Sunday News, and especially have I enjoyed the one in the issue of January 11, in which you relate your impressions of the Citadel cadets as they received their first baptism of fire at Tulifinny, as I happened to be one of the dandy-fine boys who did "stand up square to the rack" when we struck "the Yanks". In the main your accounts of the fights at Tullifinny is correct, and is quite complementary to the two companies which composed the cadet battalion, under the command of Major J.B. White, but in a few instances you are in error, which is not at all surprising, as it has been forty-nine year since those fights, and human memory is a most treacherous thing.

Aided by a pretty tenacious memory and a rereading of Major White's report, as found in Thomas's "History of the South Carolina Military Academy," on pages 205-6-7-8, I find that Capt. (afterwards Governor) Hugh S. Thompson commanded Company A and Capt. J. P. Thomas, with Lieuts. A.J. Norris and R.O. Sams, commanded Company B, and not Lieut. Huger, as you suppose; in fact, there was no Lieut Huger in either company, but C. Huger was a private in Company B. December 6 the train carrying the hospital battalion was stopped just beyond Tullifinny trestle, and against the fighting about three miles off, in the direction of Gregory's Point the noise of the rifle firing could be plainly heard, and we were marched at a double-quick in the direction of the battle, and soon the whistle of the minie balls could be heard, but none of us were hit, and when we arrived at the scene of the fight the Yankees had retired. We then fell back to the Tulifinny trestle and slept on our arms at the trestle that night.

I well recollect an incident of that night that furnished considerable amusement to all the cadets, except one. Just before a train came thundering over the trestle and Capt. B.A. Miller, of Company B, waking up suddenly and not knowing what was the matter plunged into Tulifinny Creek and got thoroughly soaked. It was a very cold night and there was a heavy frost on the ground next morning. The next day, which was December 7, we were, with the 47th Georgia, marched in the direction of the enemy in order to ascertain his exact position and determine the propriety of attacking him in his intrenched position, about three miles east of the railroad towards the coast. The entire line of skirmishers soon became engaged with those of the enemy, and steadily drove them back on their intrenchments. This skirmish lasted about three hours, Company B relieving Company A, (its ammunition having been exhausted) and the entire battalion was thus engaged in the skirmish. When the ammunition of Company A became exhausted they retired in good order, and Company B was rushed in to take their places during a brisk fire from the enemy, and many of us had forgotten whether we were No. 1 or No. 2, and there was considerable confusion along the line.

Capt. Thomas, with his sword drawn, rushed in front of us and gave the command, "Halt!" "Fall in," just as on the parade ground at the Citadel; when inline the command was given, "Front!" "Dress to the right," "Count off from the right," and then everyone double-quicked to his position on the skirmish line and leisurely retired. While all this was going on the bullets, grape and canister were whistling all around us, and it has always been a wonder to me that we were not all killed.

We then fell back to the railroad and slept that night under our arms in old broom sedge field by the side of the railroad. I remember I slept very soundly that night in that grass, with my gun by my side, and no covering except "the clouded canopy of the heavens," and next morning there was a heavy white frost all over that old field. The next day, which was the 8th, we were engaged in throwing up temporary breastworks on the east side and parallel with the railroad.

The casualties in this skirmish were as follows: Lieut Amory Coffin, severely wounded in the head; Cadet J.B. Patterson, mortally wounded, afterwards died; Cadets Joseph W. Barnwell and E.C. McCarty, severely wounded; Cadet S.F. Hollingsworth, A.J. Green, A.R. Heyward and W.A. Pringle, slightly wounded.

The next morning, which was December 9th, the enemy advanced in full force against our position on the railroad. Our position was on the left next to the 47th Georgia, on our right. Major

White acted with great coolness and daring that day. He cantered his horse up and down our line admonishing us to remain concealed behind the breastwork and hold our fire until the command to fire was given. As soon as the enemy got through the swamp in our front and emerged into the old field, where they could be seen, Major White, at the head of the battalion, rose in his stirrups and gave the command, just as if on the parade ground, "Attention battalion, Ready, aim, fire." At the command, "attention battalion," each cadet sprang to his feet, and when the command "fire" was given our three hundred rifles belched forth as one gun. The effect was instantaneous. The enemy fell back in great confusion, leaving their dead and wounded on the field. We continued firing for a while and when the command, "Cease firing" was given and the smoke lifted the enemy was nowhere to be seen.

I remember one poor fellow, an officer, was brought out on a litter through our lines, and appeared to be desperately wounded, and I think soon died. It was after this affair at the railroad that the Yankees planted a battery across the swamp in an old field and commenced shelling passing trains. We were moved into the woods on the west side of the railroad. When not on picket duty, we kept ourselves comfortable by building huge fires, where we cooked our scanty rations. It was while in these woods that W.D. Palmer was struck by solid shell in the left hand, tearing his hand into shreds. His hand was amputated just above the wrist, but he never left us, but stayed with the command till we were disbanded at Greenville. After the war he settled near St. Stephens and was successfully engaged in farming. He never married and died last year. He was as gallant a soldier as ever shouldered a gun.

I have no recollection of the North Carolina "Reserves" you mention, and am pretty sure the reference is to a militia company from Marion County (then district,) commanded by Capt. W.J. Davis. This company was composed of "elderly men" and 16 year old boys, and mustered in rank and file about 154 men. They arrived after the fights in Tulifinny and camped in the old field on the right of the railroad, just beyond Tulifinny Creek, and near to the woods, where the cadet battalion was bivouacked. They arrived soon after the Yankee battery began shelling the passing trains and knew very little of our military tactics and were encumbered with a lot of "pots, ovens, frying pans, bedding, etc," as you describe. The cadets were detailed every day to drill this disorganized mass of old men and boys, who had not even learned to change step, and when a shell from the Yankee battery would come screaming over the field it was with difficulty that discipline could be maintained.

With a number of the 16 year old boys I had gone to school in the old Marion district, and to some of them I was closely related, and I had known a number of the elderly men from my earliest recollection, and they were our most solid and respectable citizens. Five years after, I married the daughter of the fourth sergeant of this company, the late John Mace; and two uncles of my wife, Gewood and Elihu Berry, were privates in this same company. In looking over the roll of this militia from Marion, I find that all the elderly men are long since dead and a majority of the 16 year-old boys have already" crossed the river," A few, now prominent citizens of Marion, Dillon, and Florence counties still survive, among them the Hon. Jas. D. Montgomery, for years county treasurer of Marion County and member of the Constitutional Convention of 1895, and Ex- Sheriff Wm. A. Wall, of Marion; Wm. B. Allen, Neal McInis and T.C. Sherwood, of Dillon County; R.J. Rogers, Mullins, and Isham E. Watson, of Florence County.

The Citadel cadets left Tulifinny on Christmas day; 1864, and went direct to James Island, where they did picket duty, twenty-four hours on and twenty-four hours off, till the evacuation of Charleston, February 17, 1865. For a part of the time we were on James Island we had tents, and though the duty was hard and exacting, we greatly enjoyed like, living as we did in the open and drinking in the saltwater breezes.

Battle of Tulifinny

Mural by David Humphreys Miller.

My messmates on the island were John C. Tiedeman, an Ex-Alderman of the city, and J. Allen, now holding a government position in the Caston house at Charleston. Meng's father sent him down a negro man who was a fine cook. Tiedeman's father, the venerable Otto Tiedeman, kept us supplied with groceries of all kinds, while Allen's father, who was a truck farmer near the city, furnished us with vegetables fresh from the fields, and these with the rations we drew, gave us "plenty and variety." My physical condition soon became such that I could only button the top button of my cadet uniform.

On the night of the evacuation I was on picket in the lower part of the island, in the direction of Stono River. That afternoon while on vidette duty I could plainly see the men on the picket line of the enemy and could see transports and gunboats moving around. The Yankees evidently believed that the island was being evacuated, as Sherman was then in our rear at Columbia. About 9 o'clock we were quietly taken off the picket line and marched to the long bridge over the Ashley in pursuit of the main body of the battalion, which had crossed the bridge much earlier. I am pretty sure our pickets were the last to leave the island by way of the long bridge. We caught up with our command early next morning. Marching on to St. Stephens after a few days' delay, we secured transportation to Cheraw, where we got in front of Sherman. At Cheraw our battalion acted as the rear guard of the army and crossed the bridge over the Pee-Dee into Marlboro County in rear of the Cavalry. The bridge was fired before the Yankees could cross, but they ran up a battery on the hill near St. David's Church and fired at us as long as we were in range. At the crossroads, about one and one-half miles from Cheraw, we were allowed to take the first rest we had had in hours. In a few moments, though bombshells were occasionally bursting around us, I was sound asleep. We were right at a road I had often travelled in my boyhood days, and when the bugle sounded "fall in," I looked longingly down the road towards my home, thirty miles away, and took up the weary tramp, tramp, tramp to Fayetteville, N.C.

This was the beginning of the great March rains of 1865, known in all this section as the "great Sherman freshets." The rains were incessant, streams greatly swollen and the roads in a terrible condition. Arriving at Fayetteville we crossed the Cape Fear River and proceeded to Raleigh by way of Smithfield. Before reaching Raleigh the battalion was, at the request of Governor Magrath, ordered back to South Carolina. At Raleigh we got railroad transportation to Chester, S.C. by way of Greensboro and Charlotte, N.C. From Chester we marched across the country to Shelton, on Broad River, and then by rail to Spartanburg, where we took up quarters in Wofford college. It was while we were in Spartanburg that we first heard as a rumor, that Lee had surrendered. Late in April we marched to Greenville, S.C., where, on April 29, we were given a twenty days' furlough, and we all got home as best we could.

Besides those wounded at Tullifinny the following cadets died from disease: R.F. Nichols, John Culbreath, G.O. Buck, T.A. Johnson, and R. Noble. T.A. Johnson died in the Wofford College building while we were camped there. From the first we received nothing for our services, either from the state or the Confederacy, except the rations we consumed.

After the war Major White removed to Marion, where he lived till his death a few years ago, full of years and honors. For many years he taught the Marion High School, and for several terms was country school superintendent. He also worked as a civil engineer, and was a most painstaking and accurate land surveyor. He owned a small farm near the town and was the pioneer in this section of the now great strawberry business. It was at Marion that his first wife died, childless. He afterwards married the daughter of the Rev. Hugh A.C. Walker, late of the South Carolina Conference and reared and educated four noble sons, now first-class men. Some of his boys graduated at the Citadel. There was never a nobler man than Major White. Modest as a maiden, he was courageous as a lion; kind and gentle, yet he was a rigid disciplinarian; with a fine sense of humor, he was pure and chaste of speech. It was a delight to visit his home, for he was given to hospitality, and as a guest he was pleasant and entertaining. On the long march through slush and mud from Cheraw to Raleigh I have often seen him with as many guns of the boys as he could hold on the withers of his horse, and often he would dismount and walk for miles in the mud while two and sometimes three, worn-out boys were astride the old bay horse. Peace to his ashes! One of the "Dandy-Jim boys" of 1864.

John C. Sellers

Sellers, S.C. [2]

Chapter 7

Battle of Coosawhatchie

James M. Nichols wrote the following narrative concerning his observations and recollections during his service in the Federal army with the 48th New York Infantry. In 1886, he wrote "48th New York Infantry: Perry's Saints, Or the Fighting Parsons Regiment in the War of the Rebellion." In Chapter Nine, he describes his account of the attack against Coosawhatchie.

Nichols was mustered in as a second lieutenant when he enlisted at Brooklyn, New York. He participated in this battle on October 22, 1862. Since his account is based on his first-hand knowledge, I have included Chapter Nine in its entirety.

> *Expedition to Coosawhatchie. Landing at Dawson's plantation. March to Coosawhatchie. Ambuscade. Firing on Confederate train. Confederate prisoners. Destruction of track. Retreat. Peril of Lieutenant Corwin. Lieutenant Blanding wounded. Pocatalico expedition a failure. Perilous voyage back to Pulaski. Confederate weapons. Yellow fever. Death*

of General Mitchell. His character. Review of Coosawhatchie.

[October, 1862]

OCTOBER 21 we embarked on the steamer Planter, six companies of fifty men each, and proceeded to Hilton Head, where we joined the main body of troops belonging to the expedition, and, accompanied by a number of gunboats, started for the point of attack. The morning of the 22d found us opposite Mackay's Point on the Coosawhatchie River, in rear of the fleet, which numbered in all fifteen gunboats and transports. This was the point of disembarkation for the main body, but we proceeded farther up the river, accompanied by two gunboats; We had not gone far before Our boat grounded on a point on the Dawson plantation near the house, and we landed small boats. A few cavalry pickets delayed us a little, but we finally started up the road with Company H deployed as skirmishers under command of the writer.

This road led directly to the village of Coosawhatchie, and ran nearly parallel to the railroad. The attempt to skirmish through the woods was soon abandoned, owing to the dense growth of plants and shrubs and trailing vines. The Spanish bayonet plant was the most formidable, its thick bristling points presenting such obstacles to our progress that we were soon compelled to confine ourselves to an advanced position on the road. Where other roads intersected, guards were stationed. A short march brought us to an open space, with the railroad *in plain sight, only about two hundred yards distant from the turnpike. Without waiting for special orders, Company H was deployed along the railway embankment, at the same time that the whistle of an engine warned us that a train was approaching.*

Carefully posting the men along the track, but out of sight, a cautious observation discovered the train stopped a short distance below us. It was a period of anxious suspense, until we were assured that it was again in motion, when, the most careful instructions having been given as to when and how to fire, we awaited its approach. Several platform cars were loaded with troops, as we poured in our fire upon them, at only a few feet distance, the effect was terrible. In an instant those crowded masses of humanity had disappeared. Some were killed and more were wounded, but a large number jumped from the train and concealed themselves in the swamp and woods. A few were taken prisoners, but the wounded were left to be cared for by their own people, who were known to be nearby, as we had no means of caring for them.

It was a cruel ambuscade, for as they came to the place where we were awaiting them, it was apparent that they had no intimation of our presence in the vicinity. We hoped to injure the engine and so wreck the train, and a number of the most reliable men were assigned to that special duty; but it passed on out of sight, and we gave our attention to the destruction of the railroad, under the direction of the engineers who had accompanied us for such purposes.

Not much was accomplished before heavy firing warned us that we could not delay; and, collecting the prisoners and such arms as we had captured, we proceeded to join the regiment. This had arrived at the open space just in season to discharge the little cannon, which the colonel had borrowed from the navy, at the passing train, when it pushed on, hoping to destroy the bridge which crossed the river a little farther up the road; but the Confederates were found strongly entrenched, with heavy batteries guarding its approaches, and, after carefully feeling of the position and drawing the fire of the batteries, the colonel was obliged to give the order to return.

Company H was again thrown out as skirmishers, and, discovering what was supposed to be a Confederate detachment, commenced firing. Fortunately, before any injury was done, it was ascertained that it was Lieutenant Corwin with his company, which had been left to guard a threatening point. Nothing further occurred until we reached the boat, when, as we were embarking, the little knot of cavalry which had been closely watching our movements for some time rode rapidly forward and gave us a volley, by which Lieutenant Blanding, of the 3d Rhode Island Artillery, who accompanied us, was severely wounded.

A few shells from the little Parrot gun on our bow dispersed them, and we steamed down the river without further casualty. The main body of the expedition had the usual experience at Pocotaligo, where they hoped to be able to effectually destroy the railroad. The force was too small, and was repulsed with severe loss. We nevertheless expected to renew the attempt the next day; but this purpose was given up, and we were ordered back to the fort. The perils of our return passage were quite equal to any that we had encountered, for in the intense darkness the pilot lost his way, and for a long time we were buffeted about by wind and waves, not knowing what was to become of us.

The next day we had leisure to examine the weapons we had captured. It was a curious collection, consisting of rifles, swords of venerable age, and a species of cleaver, much resembling those commonly used by butchers, showing to what extremities the Home Guards, at least, were already reduced. As I write I have a specimen of the last mentioned weapon on my table, personally taken from a rebel at Coosawhatchie.

October 28, General Mitchell was reported seriously ill with yellow fever, and General Brannon assumed command of the department.

October 29, Dr. Strickland, our chaplain, an old friend of General Mitchell, was sent for to attend him. October 30, General Mitchell died, at 6 P. M. And as others at Hilton Head were prostrated with the same disease, there was danger that it would spread through the department, and every precaution was taken to guard against it. The loss of General Mitchell was a severe blow. He had the confidence of the troops, had shown his ability as a commander, and was supposed to be in such relations with the authorities at Washington as to promise such additions to our forces as would enable us to undertake something of importance.

Our last expedition would perhaps have had a better result had he been well enough to assume its direction. As it was, the colors of the Whippy Swamp Guards, with the prisoners and arms, captured by Company H of our regiment, were the only favorable results, while the complete failure of the main expedition, with the loss of so many men, added another to the disheartening blows from which the department had suffered from the beginning.

And now the loss of General Mitchell, on whom our hopes were centered, left us without a promise for the future. Soon after our return from Coosawhatchie, two deserters from the 1st Georgia regiment, called the Whippy Swamp Guards, came down from Savannah. They reported the loss of thirty men, their major, and the engineer of the train, at Coosawhatchie, together with their colors, These latter, which we had in our possession, attested the correctness of their statement in at least one particular.

Had the Confederates whom we attacked been commanded by anyone of ordinary ability, troops would have been sent down by the railroad to cut off our retreat, for there was but one road by which we could return, and this was bordered on either side by impenetrable woods, so that a small force could have held us and made our escape impossible. It is probable that our attack at the railroad so disconcerted them that before they recovered, it was too late to interrupt our rapid retreat. Those who sent us into such a trap either knew nothing of the country, or were willing to make the sacrifice of our command for the sake of drawing off troops from the main point of attack.

Looking back upon it now, it seems a part of the blundering operations which characterized our department for the most of the time that we were there, the attack on Pulaski forming a happy exception to the general rule. [1]

Commendation

General order of General Beauregard. C. S. Army.

General Orders NO 46 Headquarters Department of SC, Ga, and FL

The troops engaged in the action with the enemy at Pocotaligo on the 22d October, 1862, will have inscribed on their colors "Pocotaligo, 22d October 1862," in honor of the veteran-like steadiness and unsurpassable courage displayed on that day in their conflict with and defeat of an enemy of almost incredible superiority in numbers. The whole country has been already informed of and appreciates the brilliant events and incidents of the battle of Pocotaligo, and it has only remained thus officially to authorize an honor so brilliantly won. The Field of Pocotaligo, made memorable by those who held it on the 22d of October, 1862, surely cannot be yielded up to any greater force with which the enemy may attack in that quarter. By command of General Beauregard:

Thomas Jordan,
Chief of Staff
Coosawhatchie [2]

Chapter 8

Battle of Honey Hill

The Battle of Honey Hill was the third battle of Major General William T. Sherman's *March to the Sea*. It was fought on November 30, 1864. It did not include Sherman's main force, marching from Atlanta to Savannah, Georgia. Sherman ordered Major General John G. Foster to attack and cut off the Charleston Savannah railroad to prevent the Confederate troops from using it. Foster planned to move his forces on November 28 and strike the railroad depot at Gopher Hill (now Ridgeland).

However, due to an injury, Foster transferred the field command to Brigadier General John P. Hatch.

According to Wikipedia,

> *Hatch's force left Hilton Head on November 28. It consisted of 5,000 men—two brigades of the Coast Division of the Department of the South, one naval brigade, and portions of three batteries of light artillery. They steamed up the Broad River in transports to cut the Railroad at Pocotaligo. Due to a heavy fog the troops were not disembarked from*

> the transports until late the following afternoon, and Hatch immediately started forward to cut the railroad near Grahamville.
>
> However, the expedition maps and guides proved worthless and Hatch was unable to proceed on the right road until the morning of November 30. At Honey Hill, a few miles from Grahamville, he encountered a Confederate force of regulars and militia, under Col. Charles J. Colcock, with a battery of seven guns across the road.

Determined attacks were launched by U.S. Colored Troops including a brigade led by *Alfred S. Hartwell* that included the *54th Massachusetts* and *55th Massachusetts. The position of the Federal force was such that only one section of artillery could be used at a time, and the Confederates were too well entrenched to be dislodged. Fighting kept up until dark when Hatch, realizing the impossibility of successfully attacking or turning the flank of the enemy, withdrew to his transports at Boyd's Neck, having lost 89 men killed, 629 wounded, and 28 missing. The Confederate casualties amounted to eight killed and 39 wounded.* [1]

Hatch made a report in December 1864 in which he summarized the Union losses:

- 1st Brigade: casualties of 2 officers and 54 men killed; 28 officers and 409 men wounded; 1 officer and 14 men missing.
- 2nd Brigade: casualties of 3 officers and 28 men killed; 10 officers and 160 men wounded; 1 officer and eight men missing.

- Naval Brigade: casualties of 1 man killed; 7 men wounded; 4 men missing
- Artillery Brigade: casualties of 1 officer killed; 2 officers and 12 men wounded

Cavalry: casualties of 1 man wounded

Lt Col C.C. Jones reported the Confederate losses in his *Siege of Savannah* as four killed and 40 wounded. [2]

Georgia Militia

The Georgia Militia, commanded by General G.W. Smith, had enlisted to serve the Confederacy only in Georgia. However, they marched to Grahamville at the end of November 1864 to help defend the Charleston Savannah Railroad.

In his excellent book, *Historical Sketch And Roster Of The South Carolina 3rd Cavalry Regiment,* John C. Rigdon writes,

> *There they fought gallantly November 30th, in the battle of Honey Hill, beating back the repeated Federal attacks. General Smith in his report particularly commended the service of Colonel Willis, commanding First brigade of Georgia militia; Major Cook, commanding the Athens and Augusta battalions of reserves; and Lieutenant Colonel Edwards, commanding the Forty-seventh Georgia regiment. After this brilliant affair the Georgia militia returned to the State.*
>
> Rigdon continues, *A notable feature of this battle was the presence in the ranks of the Confederates of some boy volunteers, even under the age of*

conscription. Some of those boys were not tall enough to shoot over the parapet. But they curiously and enterprisingly so arranged that one would get up on his hands and knees, making a bench on which another would stand, deliver his fire and then change places with his comrade, so that he in turn might get a shot at 'Yankees.' [3]

The "Friction and Fog of War" quickly destroyed the Union plans for 29 November. Early morning fog delayed the start of the convoy and hampered efforts to locate and land at Boyd's Landing. Once ashore, the Union's lack of accurate maps coupled with inept (or devious) local guides lead to aimless marching and counter-marching throughout the day. Union soldiers, sailors and marines marched up to fifteen miles during the day and into the night only to advance a total of three miles toward the railroad, ending the day still seven miles short of their objective. The Coast Division had missed its best opportunity to reach the Savannah and Charleston Railroad virtually unopposed.

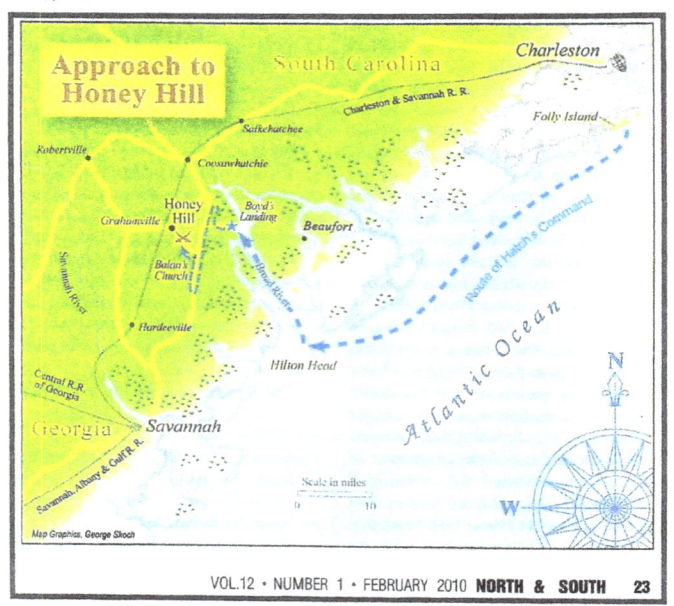

The Confederate Response
Fortune smiled on the Confederates throughout the 29th since the only units available to oppose the Union's 5,500-man Coast Division were small vedettes of the *3rd SC Cavalry* (246 men) dispersed to guard possible landing sites and four batteries of artillery (415 men) deployed to guard the three avenues of approach to Grahamville. The Confederates used this reprieve to organize a defensive force to oppose the Union incursion.

Approach to Honey Hill

North & South Magazine. Vol. 12. Number 1. February 2010. Page 23.

United States Colored Troops (USCT) at Honey Hill

Thousands of African American men in the Federal regiments of the United States Colored Troops were at the Battle of Honey Hill. The 54th and 55th Massachusetts came from Charleston, the 32nd USCT from Hilton Head, the 34th and 35th from Jacksonville, Florida, and the 102nd from Beaufort.

During the battle, the 54th Massachusetts un-intentionally got mixed in with the white 144th New York and 25th Ohio. This was a rare occurrence of black and white Federal troops fighting side by side.

When the color sergeant for the 55th was killed, Corporal Andrew Smith picked up the colors and carried them for the remainder of the battle. He was later awarded the Congressional Medal of Honor. The gallant and courageous charge by the black troops lasted only about ten minutes. Two-thirds of the 55th had been killed or wounded when it was over.

When the 3rd New York Artillery withdrew, they could only bring one of their guns. The white officers ordered the 102nd USCT to retrieve the remaining artillery. They did so without using draft animals, pulling the guns by their hands while under heavy Confederate fire. Lt. Orson W. Bennett also received the Medal of Honor for dragging one of the heavy guns one hundred yards under intense enemy fire. General Hatch then ordered a regiment by regiment retreat back to Boyd's Landing on the morning of December 1st.

Some days later, when Confederate officers were reviewing the battlefield, one stated he had "never seen such evidence of terrible havoc from artillery." A Lieutenant named Zealy remarked the Federal corpses "lay five deep dead as a mackerel."

Three soldiers from the 54th Massachusetts USCT were captured. Two of them were executed. The third, an escaped slave, was returned to his South Carolina owner.

The Federal white bodies were buried in shallow graves. The black soldiers were left unburied. Tradition states that some planters brought their slaves to see the gruesome scene to persuade them not to escape to the Federal lines.

Source: "Bittersweet: Black Virginians in Blue at the Battle of Honey Hill." [4]

Confederate Account of the Battle

The *Savannah Republican* Newspaper reported the Confederate account of the Battle of Honey Hill on December 3, 1864,

> *In our account of this affair, in Thursday morning's issue, we spoke of it as a "drawn battle," both armies having continued the fight until dark. We wrote with the official dispatch of Gen. SMITH before us, in which his modesty, which is equal to his merit, led us into error by withholding the true character of the contest and the real magnitude of the victory, for such it was, and, for the numbers engaged, one of the most brilliant and important of the war. It was clearly a movement on the part of the enemy to cooperate with SHERMAN; so large a force would never have been sent simply to cut the Charleston Railroad, when the Yankees believed it to be defended only by a company of cavalry.*

Honey Hill is about two and a half miles east of the village of Grahamsville, Beaufort District. On the crest of this, where the road or highway strikes it, is a semi-circular line of earthworks, defective, though, in construction, as they are too high for infantry, and have little or no exterior slope. These works formed the center of our lines on Wednesday, while our left reached up into the pinelands without protection, and our right along the line of fence that skirts the swamp below the batteries. They commanded fully the road in front as it passes through the swamp at the base of the hill, and only some fifty or sixty yards distant. Through the swamp, during the winter months, runs a small creek, which spreads up and down the road for some thirty or forty yards, but is quite shallow the entire distance. Some sixty yards beyond this creek the main road turns off to the left, making an obtuse angle, while another and smaller road makes off to the right from the same point.

The enemy came by the former road and turned the angle apparently before they were aware of the preserve of an opposing force. They consisted of four regiments of whites and the same number of blacks. Prisoners, of which ten or twelve are in our possession, state that this force was commanded by Gens. POTTER and HATCH; some of them say Gen. FOSTER was also present as chief of command. The negroes, as usual, formed the advance, and nearly reached the creek when our batteries opened upon them down the road with a terrible volley of spherical case. This threw them into temporary confusion, but the entire force, estimated at five thousand, was quickly restored to order, and thrown into a line of battle parallel with our own, up and down the margin of the swamp. Thus the battle raged from 11 A.M. till dark. The enemy's center and left were most exposed, and suffered terribly. Their right was posted behind an old dam that ran through an old swamp, and it maintained its position till the close of the fight. Our left was very much exposed, and an attempt was once or twice made by the enemy to turn it by advancing through the swamp and up the hill, but they were driven back without a prolonged struggle.

The center and left of the enemy fought with a desperate earnestness. Several attempts were made to charge our batteries, and many got nearly across the swamp, but were, in every instance, forced back by the galling fire poured into them from our lines. We made a visit to the field the day following, and found the swamp and road literally strewn with their dead. Some eight or ten bodies were floating in the water where the road crosses, and in a ditch on the roadside just beyond, we saw six negroes piled one on top of the other. A Colonel of one of the negro regiments, with his horse, was killed whilst fearlessly leading his men across the creek in a charge. With that exception, all the dead and wounded officers were carried off by the enemy during the night. Many traces were left where they were dragged from the woods to the road and thrown into ambulances or carts. We counted some sixty or seventy bodies in the space of about an acre many of which were horribly mutilated by shells some with half their hands shot off, and others completely disemboweled. The artillery was served with great accuracy, and we doubt if any battle-field of the war presents such havoc among the trees and shrubbery. Immense pines and other growth were cut short off or torn into shreds.

From all indications it is estimated that the loss of the enemy is fully five or six hundred. This is the lowest estimate that we have heard. Many officers are of the opinion that their loss cannot be less than one thousand. Ours was eight killed outright and thirty-nine wounded, three or four mortally. The enemy fought to some disadvantage, as they fired uphill and most of their shots ranged too high.

Our infantry behaved with the greatest valor. Throughout the protracted struggle, there was little or no straggling, nearly every man standing firmly to his post of duty. The Georgia Brigade was commanded by Col. WILLIS, whose behavior on the field is highly commendable. The Athens Battalion, under Maj. COOK, and Augusta Battalion. Maj. JACKSON, stood manfully to their work. The South Carolina Artillery also acted most handsomely, and served their guns with the skill of veterans. Great praise is bestowed by the ranking officers on Capt. STEWART, of the Beaufort Artillery (five guns,) and on EARLE'S and KANAPAUX'S batteries, each of which had a gun in action.

As before stated, the general command was vested in Major-Gen. GUSTAVUS SMITH, of the Georgia

State forces, though the line was immediately under the direction of Col. COLCOCK, whose conduct on the occasion is spoken of as beyond all praise. The gallant Col. GONZALES was an active participant in the fight, and might have been seen everywhere along the line posting the guns and encouraging the troops.

So much for the battle of Honey Hill. The enemy were whipped long before its close, but they waited for night to save themselves from disaster in their retreat. Soon after dark they made off with all possible speed, and, as the evidences show, with the wildest fright and confusion. Nearly everything was thrown away in their flight. The road and woods for miles was strewed with clothing of every description, canteens, cooking utensils, etc., etc., whilst in their camp, about two miles from the battle-field, they left everything. Any quantity of provisions, bottles of liquor, preserved meats, blankets, overcoats, etc., were abandoned in their hasty retreat. With the exception of shelling from their gunboats next day, which was harmless, nothing has been heard of them since their galling defeat and inglorious flight. [5]

Federal Account of the Battle

The Federal perspective of the Battle of Honey Hill was quite different from the Confederacy's view. The following reports of Federal Major General John G. Foster and Brigadier General John P. Hatch are included in *The War of the Rebellion: Official Records of the Civil War*. I obtained them online from The Ohio State University's Department of History. [6]

Numbers 1. Reports of Major General John G. Foster, U. S. Army, commanding Department of the South, including operations November 28-December 7.

HEADQUARTERS DEPARTMENT OF THE SOUTH,
STEAMER NEMAHA,
Tulifinny River, December 7, 1864.

GENERAL: I have the honor to report that I left Hilton Head on the night of November 28 for Boyd's Neck, on the south side of Broad River, with all the disposable troops in this department, amounting to 5,000 infantry, cavalry, and artillery, with 500 sailors and marines. Owing to a thick fog and the incapacity of our pilots many of the boats lost their way and others grounded, so that the troops did not get ashore until late in the afternoon of the 29th. I then placed Brigadier-General Hatch in command of the force with orders to push forward and cut the railroad. He marched at once, but the maps and guides proved totally worthless, and after being twice misguided the troops reached the right road by morning. Thence, after daylight, they advanced toward Grahamville through a densely wooded country, driving back the enemy's artillery and infantry to a rise of ground called Honey Hill, a short distance this side of Grahamville, where they met a battery across the road, with seven guns. The enemy's infantry, rather over 4,000 and nearly equal to our own in number, was posted behind entrenchments in the woods on each side of the road. This position was immediately attacked with *vigor and determination, but from the unfavorable nature of the ground, which admitted the employment of only one section of our artillery, we were unable to drive off the enemy, who did not, however, venture to advance beyond his entrenchments. After an obstinate fight of several hours, General Hatch, finding that the enemy's line could be neither successfully assaulted nor outflanked, retired after dark to a strong position about two miles and a half from Boyd's Neck. The rebels made no attempt to follow. Our loss was 88 killed, 623 wounded (149 of whom so slightly as not to be sent to the hospital), and 43 missing.*

From November 30 to December 5, while keeping the greater part of the force at Boyd's Neck, I made at different points, with the assistance of the navy, several demonstrations- in one of which the Twenty-fifth Regiment Ohio Volunteer Infantry marched six miles into the interior toward Pocataligo and captured two pieces of artillery at Church Bridge, near Gardner's Corners, one of which the men dragged off by hand. On the night of December 5 I embarked a force under command of Brigadier-General Potter. From Boyd's Neck proceeded, at daylight, to Tulifinny Creek, and landed the men at James Gregory's plantation, on the right bank, in pontoons and launches. General Potter pushed immediately forward, and about one miles a half out met the enemy, whom he forced rapidly back to the spot where the road up the peninsula between the Coosawhatchie and Tulifinny meets the road running across from one river to the other. Here the rebels, being re-enforced from the south side of the Coosawhatchie, made a stand and attacked our left vigorously, but our men repulsed them handsomely, capturing a battle-flag and some prisoners, and got possession of the crossing, which we now firmly hold. A detachment sent to the right destroyed the road bridge over the Tulifinny. Our loss in the whole affair was about 5 killed and 50 wounded. The railroad is less than three-quarters of a mile from our front, separated by a dense wood, through which is only a bridle path, and in the skirt of which are our pickets. I have ordered nearly all the force from Boyd's Neck to this position, and also some 30-pounder Parrotts, with which we can reach the railroad, even should our men not succeeded in gaining it, as I hope they may, as also the bridge over the Coosawhatchie. Our position is strong, the spirit of the troops excellent, and the landings and means of communication good. The naval force, under orders from Admiral Dahlgren, nave co-operated cordially and efficiently both by water and land. The reports received from prisoners and deserters relative to General Sherman's movements are very conflicting. A lieutenant who deserted on the 4th reports that General Sherman was in sight of Savannah. There can be no doubt that he is nearing Savannah, as all the deserters and prisoners who have recently come in agree that troops are leaving Charleston and Augusta for Savannah.

Very respectfully, your obedient servant,

J. G. FOSTER,
Major-General, Commanding.

*Major General H. W. HALLECK, U. S. Army,
Chief of Staff, Armies of United States,
Washington, D. C.*

Numbers 2. *Report of Brigadier General John P. Hatch, U. S. Army, commanding Coast Division. HDQRS. COAST DIVISION, DEPARTMENT OF THE SOUTH, Deveaux's Neck, S. C., December -, 1864.*

CAPTAIN: I have the honor to make the following report of the movements of this division from the date of its embarkation at Hilton Head to the close of the action at Honey Hill:

The force collected from different points in the Department of the South, with the addition of a small brigade from the navy, numbered, including all arms, about 5,500 men, organized as follows: Two brigades of infantry, commanded by Brigadier General E. E. Potter and Colonel A. S. Hartwell, Fifty-fifth Massachusetts Volunteers; Naval Brigade, Commander George H. Preble, U. S. Navy, commanding; portions of three batteries light artillery, Lieutenant Colonel William Ames, Third Rhode Island Artillery, commanding. It was embarked on the evening of the 28th November, with the intention of landing at Boyd's Neck at daylight the following morning. My command of the force was to commence after landing. At 2. 30 a. m., the hour previously designated, the signal for sailing was given from the flagship of the department commander. The transports immediately got underway; but soon after, a dense fog covering the river, some came to anchor, others continuing the advance grounded, whilst others, by a mistake of the pilots, were taken up the Cacaos instead of the Broad River. The pilot of my own steamer advising me to wait daylight, I did so, and consequently it was from that transport the first troops commenced landing, at about 11 a. m. The steamer Canonicus, containing engineer troops and material, was unfortunately one of the transports that had gone up the Cacaos by mistake, and did not arrive at Boyd's Neck until about 2 p. m. This caused a delay in building the necessary landing to enable the artillery and means of transportation to be dis-embarked. The Naval Brigade was the first organized body landed.

It was immediately pushed to the front to occupy a crossroads two miles in advance of the landing. Attached to this brigade was a battery of eight light guns, drawn by sailors. The brigade met and drove toward Bee's Creek a small force of the enemy. The Thirty-second U. S. Colored Troops, as soon as landed, was sent to the support of the brigade. At 4 p. m. the detachment of cavalry and a large portion of Potter's brigade having landed, I determined to push forwarded immediately and attempt to seize the railroad at Grahamville, without waiting the landing of the artillery and the remainder of the infantry. The debarkation of the remainder of the troops continued through the night and following day as the transports arrived. Unfortunately the maps and guides proved equally worthless. The Naval Brigade had pushed back the enemy, who, retreating toward Bee's Creek, were followed two miles from the cross-roads in a direction opposite

The Civil War In My South

to the route we were to march, supposing in the direct road to Grahamville. Potter's brigade followed, and it was not until the latter had overtaken the Naval Brigade that the error was discovered. The troops countermarched and returned to the crossroads. The sailors dragging the artillery were found to be worn out, and the Naval Brigade was left at that point, with orders to come up in the morning. We then pushed on with Potter's brigade and the cavalry. Two miles from the crossroads was found a fork in the road near a church. The guide, pretending to recognize the point, led the column on the left-hand road. Four miles beyond the church it became evident, that the guide had mistaken the road, and I returned to the church, where we bivouacked at 2. a. m. The men had marched fifteen miles, had been up most of the previous night, had worked hard during the day, and were unable to march farther. The distance marched, if upon the right road, would have carried us to the railroad, and I have since learned we would have met, at that time, little or no opposition.

On the morning of the 30th of Artillery and Naval Brigades having come up, it was reported to me that horses had been furnished the naval battery, except for two mountains howitzers. These I directed to return to and hold the cross-roads, supported by four companies of the Fifty-fourth Massachusetts Volunteers. They were attacked, and repulsed a body of the enemy from the direction of Bee's Creek battery. I then marched on the direct road toward Grahamville in the following order: Cavalry; Potter's brigade, with Mesereau's battery, Third New York Artillery; Naval Brigade; Titus battery, Third New York Artillery; and all of Hartwell's brigade that had arrived at the point, consisting of one regiment and two companies of a second. At 9. 15 a. m. met the advance of the enemy, consisting of two pieces of artillery with an infantry support. Our column was marching in a narrow road with dense woods on both sides. The action was opened by General Potter, who advanced the One hundred and twenty-seventh New York Volunteers as skirmishers, supported by the Twenty-fifth Ohio and the One hundred and forty-fourth and One hundred and fifty-seventh New York Volunteers. The supports were deployed on the sides of the road when the country opened sufficiently to allow it. Hartwell's brigade was also brought forward as soon it could find open ground on the right side of the road. We advanced gradually, driving the enemy about three miles and a half, their artillery being silenced at every opening of the section with our advance. Our casualties were not severe during this advance, but a valuable and gallant officer, First Lieutenant Edward A. Wildt, Third New York Artillery, fell mortally wounded whilst sighting one of his guns. At 11 a. m. the head of the column came unexpectedly of the main body of the enemy in position. At this point the road bends to the left. The advance following it found themselves in front of an inclosed work pierced for four guns.

The redoubt, situated on the crest of a small ridge, was the center of the enemy's line. It is said to have been built two years since, although until now unknown to us. Following the crest of the hill on either side the redoubt, the enemy had thrown up a line of rifle-pits, and within these waited with seven pieces of artillery our attack. In front of the enemy's line ran a small creek, bounded by a marsh covered with dense undergrowth. This was not impassable, but presented a serious obstacle to our advance, being completely commanding by the enemy's fire. Potter's brigade was quickly formed in line of battle parallel to that of the enemy. One section of Mesereau's artillery, placed in position in the road, opened fire upon the redoubt. The left of Potter's brigade re-enforced by two companies of the Fifty-fourth Massachusetts Volunteers and part of the Fifty-fifth Massachusetts Volunteers, which had by mistake taken position on the left of the road-made two desperate attacks on the main work of the enemy, led by Colonel A. S. Hartwell, commanding Second Brigade. They were repulsed with severe loss. The Fifty-fifth Massachusetts Volunteers were rallied, and, with the Marine Battalion, sent to the support of the right wing of the line of battle, with orders to turn left flank of the enemy. They advanced gallantly, but were unable to carry the entrenchments. This wing finally fell back a short distance to take advantage of an inequality of the ground, which gave them a position from which they repulsed several attacks made by the enemy. Charges made on our left flank were repulsed with ease. Between 1 and 2 p. m. the One hundred and second U. S. Colored Troops reached the field, having arrived at the landing at 11 a. m.

The ammunition of the troops engaged being nearly expended, and none arriving from the rear, this regiment was necessarily held in reserve, as I received information from deserters and prisoners that large re-enforcements were being received by the enemy by railroad. One section of Mesereau' artillery, having been placed in battery in a position completely commanded by the artillery and sharpshooters of the enemy, lost two of its officers wounded, and most of its horses and cannoneers; two of the ammunition-chests on the limbers were blown up. A detail of a company from the One hundred and second U. S. Colored Troops was ordered to bring off the guns. Captain A. E. Lindsay, commanding the company, was killed, and Lieutenant H. H. Alvord was severely wounded. The command of the company devolved upon a sergeant, who did not understand the object of the advance, and failed to accomplish it. First Lieutenant O. W. Bennette, One hundred and second U. S. Colored Troops, thirty men was detached for the same purpose, and executed it in the coolest and most gallant manner. Mesereau's artillery was then sent to the rear, and Titus' battery brought into action. The artillery fire was directed to be continued slowly, as the ammunition was being expended and none received from the rear. The caissons as fast as emptied were ordered to the landing to refill. About 3 p. m. 6,000 rounds of musket ammunition was received and issued to those regiments entirely out. It was, however, not certain that the enemy's position could not be carried; and whilst a moderate fire was kept up, arrangements were commenced for retiring as soon as it became dark. The ammunition of Titus' battery, except twenty-rounds each for two guns, being expended, the naval guns under Lieutenant Commander Matthews were brought, into action one section at a time. The ambulances having been landed commenced reaching the front. One section of Titus' battery, supported by two regiments of infantry, took post half a mile in the rear. Two regiments of infantry were then drawn from the flanks and posted one mile farther to the rear, where the road crossed a ravine. Two regiments of infantry were detailed to carry the wounded. At dusk the retreat commenced. The Naval Brigade, with the exception of its two pieces of artillery, then engaged, was ordered to occupy the crossroads; the One hundred and twenty-seventh New York Volunteers and One hundred and second U. S. Colored Troops, with one section naval artillery, remained at the front, keeping up a slow fire with artillery until 7. 30 p. m., when, the main body of the command being well on its march, they withdrew, and were in their turn covered by the First-sixth and One hundred and forty-fourth Regiments New York Volunteers; these were again covered by the Twenty-fifth Ohio and One hundred and fifty-seventh New York Volunteers, posted as before mentioned. The whole retrograde movement was executed without loss or confusion; there was no pursuit by the enemy or alarm of any kind; not a wounded was left on the field, except those who fell at the foot of the enemy's works in the charges in which we were repulsed; no stores or equipments fell into the hands of the enemy, except some thrown away by the men on the advance, to enable them the better to follow the enemy in his retreat.

In closing this report I must give the gallant men the credit due them. The list of killed and wounded, none of whom fell in retreat, attest their good conduct. The affair was a repulse owing entirely to the strong position held by the enemy and our want of ammunition. A few instances of individual gallantry that have come particularly to my knowledge I will mention: Colonel A. S. Hartwell, Fifty-fifth Massachusetts Volunteers, commanding brigade, received his third wound during the engagement at the foot of the enemy's entrenchments; Colonel James C. Beecher, Thirty-fifth U. S. Colored Troops, twice wounded, refused to go until the close of the action; Lieutenant George H. Crocker, Third New York Artillery, continued to serve his guns, after losing an eye, until they were withdrawn by order.

Lieutenant Cols. W. T. Bennett and James F. Hall, of my staff; S. L. Woodford, One hundred and twenty-seventh New York Volunteers; N. Haughton, Twenty-fifth Ohio; James C. Carmichael, One hundred and fifty-seventh New York Volunteers; A. J. Williard, Thirty-fifth U. S. Colored Troops; Lieutenant Commanders A. F. Crossman and E. O. Matthews, U. S. Navy; Captain T. J. Mesereau, Third

New York Artillery, Lieutenant G. G. Stoddard, U. S. Marines; Lieutenant E. H. Titus and George C. Breck, Third New York Artillery, deserve particular mention. The brigade commanders- Brigadier General E. E. Potter, Commander G. H. Preble, U. S. Navy, and Lieutenant Colonel William Ames, Third Rhode Island Artillery-gave me a hearty support. General Potter, who commanded the advance, handled his troops handsomely, and personally superintended the withdrawal of the rear of the command on the retreat. To my own staff I am indebted for their energy and activity. Colonel G. A. Pierce, quartermaster, volunteer aide, was wounded whilst making a reconnaissance. Captain G. E. Gouraud, of General Foster's staff, won the praise of all, and is particularly commended for gallantry. * Capts. W. W. Sampson, acting aide-de-camp, and T. L. Appleton, assistant provost-marshal; Lieutenant L. B. Perry, acting assistant adjutant-General; E. B. Van Winkle, aide-de-camp; D. D. McMartin, aide-de-camp, and T. C. Vidal, signal officer, did their duty nobly, and assisted in rallying at the front and leading forward those troops who, unable to stand the terrible fire of the enemy, were repulsed in the assault.

In the reports of brigade commanders, herewith inclosed, you will find personal mention of other officers. The medical department, under direction of Surg. George S. Burton, Third Rhode Island Artillery, proved itself highly efficient, and the corps of stretcher-bearer visited thoroughly all parts of the field where the troops were engaged. A list of the casualties accompanies this report. The total killed, wounded, and missing is 746. Of the 28 missing, I have been indirectly informed that 13 unwounded and 5 wounded men are in the hands of the enemy.

I am, captain, very respectfully, your obedient servant,

JNO P. HATCH,

Brigadier-General, Commanding. [6]

Chapter 9

Battle of Bentonville

Great Grandfather George fought in his last battle on April 26, 1865. It took place near the village of Bentonville, North Carolina. It was the final battle between Union Maj. Gen. William T. Sherman and Confederate Gen. Joseph E. Johnston.

> In 2006, Ronnie W. Faulkner wrote the *Battle of Bentonville* for the Encyclopedia of North Carolina:
>
> *The most significant Civil War land engagement in North Carolina, the Battle of Bentonville, occurred during 19-21 Mar. 1865 in rural Johnston County. The encounter was one of the Confederacy's last attempts to defeat the Union army before the South capitulated. With reports that Maj. Gen. William T. Sherman's 60,000-man army was marching toward Goldsboro in two columns, Gen. Joseph E. Johnston concentrated about 21,000 men near the community of Bentonville. His aim was to defeat the Union left wing before it could be reinforced by the right. Johnston thus hoped to prevent or*

delay Sherman's junction with Maj. Gen. John M. Schofield›s Federal forces at Goldsboro.

Confederate cavalry skirmished with Federal troops on 18 March, impeding their advance while Johnston moved toward Bentonville from Smithfield and Averasboro. On 19 March Johnston deployed his troops in a sickle-shaped formation across and above the Goldsboro road. On the left was Gen. Braxton Bragg's command, Hoke's Division, which included the 17- and 18-year-olds of the North Carolina Junior Reserves; it was the largest brigade in Johnston's army. On the right were the troops led by Lt. Gen. William J. Hardee, most of them veterans of the Army of Tennessee.

An engraving from *Frank Leslie's Illustrated Newspaper*, April 22, 1865, showing Bentonville the morning after the battle. North Carolina Collection, University of North Carolina at Chapel Hill Library.

On the morning of 19 March, Confederate cavalry was again attacked by advancing Union foragers but repulsed them. At 7:00 a.m. the Union left wing under Maj. Gen. Henry W. Slocum began to advance, but it soon encountered the same Confederate cavalry that had stalled the foraging details. Acting on a false report that the main Confederate force was near Raleigh, the Union left wing brushed aside the cavalry and then came under heavy fire. After the Confederates repulsed a Union probing attack, three gray-clad deserters came through the Union lines and informed Slocum that he was confronting Johnston's entire army. Undeceived, Slocum decided to dig in and summon reinforcements, a portion of which arrived by 2:00 p.m. In Johnston's words, his troop deployments "consumed a weary time," so the Confederate attack did not begin until 3:15 p.m. One Union officer stated that "the onward sweep of the rebel lines was like the waves of the ocean, resistless." The Federal left broke and fell back in confusion. Instead of taking advantage of the gaps in the remaining Federal lines, the Confederate units either attempted a frontal assault or became disorganized and failed to attack at all. During the attacks, however, fresh Union troops came up to meet them. Reinforcements likewise bolstered the collapsed Federal left, which had fallen back to a position anchored by four Union batteries. After several determined strikes failed to budge the Federal defenders, the Confederates withdrew to their original lines at sundown.

When word of the battle reached Sherman late on 19 March, he sent the Union right wing under Maj. Gen. Oliver O. Howard to Slocum's support. Johnston redeployed his lines into a V to prevent being outflanked and to guard his only route of retreat. By 4:00 p.m. on 20 March, most of the Union right wing had reached Bentonville. Johnston was forced to deploy cavalry on his flanks to give the appearance of a strong front. Uncertain of Johnston›s strength, Sherman decided against a general attack and instead ordered his subordinates to probe the Confederate defensive line. The Federal commander expected Johnston to retreat under cover of darkness, but dawn the next day revealed that the Confederates still held their entrenchments.

There was more intense skirmishing on 21 March despite the onset of heavy rain. During the afternoon, a Union attack nearly cut off Johnston's line of retreat before being repulsed by a hastily mounted Confederate counterattack. The Rebels thus escaped from Bentonville mainly because Sherman did not launch a general assault. That night the Confederates withdrew, removing as many of the wounded as possible, and returned to Smithfield. Lt. Gen. Wade Hampton's cavalry was ordered to cover the retreat, engaging in lively skirmishing with the Union forces. Total casualties at Bentonville were 1,527 Federals and 2,606 Confederates. After the battle, Sherman resumed the Union march toward Goldsboro, arriving there on 23 March. [1]

Chapter 10

Hampton's Legion

Wade Hampton, III, was born in Charleston on March 28, 1818, at 54 Hasell Street. Both of his parents were wealthy, and his life was one of privilege. He was a graduate of South Carolina College (now the University of South Carolina). He studied the law but never practiced it. When he completed his education, his father gave him the responsibility of managing the family's plantations in South Carolina and Mississippi.

In *Overlooked and Overskilled: Rebel General Hampton,* Billy Moncure writes,

> *Although Hampton had originally opposed secession in the South Carolina legislature, he decided to back his state's decision. He resigned his seat in the legislature and enlisted as a private to fight for Dixie.*
>
> *However, the Governor felt that he deserved an officer's commission, and convinced him to accept the rank of Colonel. Although it was unusual for a*

man with no military education or experience to immediately become an officer, there were several reasons for this decision.

Wade Hampton III during the Civil War

From Wikimedia Commons. Public Domain.

First off, the political class of South Carolina did not want one of their own to be seen as a lowly private. Second, as a plantation owner and legislator, he had some leadership experience. Finally, the South desperately needed money for weapons and payments to soldiers, and Hampton could fund his own legion. Hampton was happy to live up to this expectation, and financed six companies of infantry, four companies of cavalry, and an artillery battery. [1]

In early 1861, Colonel Hampton organized his legion at his Woodlands plantation home in Columbia. It was located at what is now known as Columbia's Hampton Hill area on US Highway 378.

In *A Chronological History of the Hampton Legion Battalion of Cavalry,* Ron Crawley writes,

> *The Legion began to form at Camp Hampton located three miles east of Columbia, SC at Hampton's Woodlands Plantation on May 20. The Edgefield and Brook's troops arrived June 10 and the latter welcomed the BDT (Beaufort District Troops) on their arrival some days later. After a few days, the horses and men were individually inspected by Colonel Hampton, Lt. Colonel Johnson, and Colonel John Preston. Some of those few who were rejected for unsuitable mounts were directed to obtain new mounts. The old racetrack served as the drill field where "severe" drills (5 times a day for up to 9 hours) were held under the supervision of Lt. Colonel Johnson. A "ditch and bar" type of jump was erected for the cavalry to practice at. Dress parades were conducted each evening although some of the troopers may not have yet had uniforms. Food was plentiful; beef prepared by the plantation slaves, vegetables supplied by the Hampton's and other prominent families, and bread brought in from Columbia. Laundry was taken to Millwood plantation.*
>
> *The Infantry and Artillery companies left for Virginia on June 26th while the cavalry companies waited on recruits who had not yet obtained horses. The Brook's Troop departed on June 28 and the BDT on*

June 29th (it is unknown when the Edgefield Troop left but it would have been no more than two days later). Some men from these troops as well as the entire Congaree Troop were left behind to find mounts. The cavalry traveled on the Charlotte Railroad through Greensboro and Raleigh en route to Petersburg, VA where they disembarked and were treated to a dinner courtesy of the local citizens. From here they marched the 19 miles to Richmond and moved to the "old Rocketts", a fairgrounds east of the city on the James River where the Legion was encamped.

Wade Hampton Monument on the South Carolina State House Grounds

This equestrian statue by Frederick W. Ruckstull was erected on the grounds of the S.C. State Capitol in Columbia in 1906. *Frederick Wellington Ruckstull, Fougerousse, M.J.L. (December 16, 2017). Wade Hampton-via siris-artinventories.si,edu Library Catalog.* Retrieved November 23, 2021.

Colonel Hampton and the remaining infantry joined the rest of the Legion at Camp Manning on July 4. On the first Sunday after their arrival, the Legion was inspected by President Jefferson Davis during a dress parade on July 8. During their stay the Legion was recognized as the elite of regiments and their dress parades became known as a fashionable affair. Colonel Hampton maintained strict discipline in camp, much to the displeasure of some, and the men were restricted to camp. [2]

Hampton had a distinguished military career. But, it was not without personal pain and sacrifice. His brother, Frank Hampton, was killed on June 9, 1863, during the Battle of Brandy Station. Wade was wounded during the same battle. He suffered four more wounds during the war.

I suspect the most challenging day of Hampton's service occurred on October 27, 1864. His youngest son, T. Preston Hampton, and his oldest son, Wade Hampton, IV, served on their father's staff. The general had dispatched Preston to deliver a message. After failing to return when expected, General Hampton and Wade IV searched for him. They found him on the ground, mortally wounded. Preston died soon after that. [3]

Hampton returned to South Carolina after the war and resumed his political aspirations. He served as Governor from 1877 to 1879. He resigned in 1879 to become a United States Senator. On April 11, 1902, Hampton died and was buried at the Trinity Episcopal Churchyard in Columbia.

Legion Officers, Assignments, and Battles

Officers

Colonel: Wade Hampton, III

Executive Officers: Lt. Colonel Benjamin Johnson, Lt. Colonel James Griffin

Troop Captains: Captain Matthew C Butler, Captain Clark, Captain John F Lanneau, Captain Thomas Screven, and Captain Thomas Taylor.

Cavalry Commanding Officers: Major James Griffin and Major MC Butler.

Assignments

Organized as a three-company battalion under the command of Major Matthew Caldwell Butler.

Company A Edgefield Hussars (Edgefield), Company B Brooks Troop (Greenville), and

Company C Beaufort District Troop (Greenville). June 12, 1861.

Company D Congaree Troop (Columbia) was added to the battalion. The Legion reunited in August at Brentville, near Manassas Junction. August 5, 1861.

Assigned to Cavalry Brigade, Army of Northern Virginia. June-July 1862.

Assigned to Hampton's Brigade, Cavalry Division, Army of Northern Virginia. July 1862.

Consolidated with the 4th South Carolina Cavalry Battalion and two other companies to form the 2nd South Carolina Cavalry Regiment. August 22, 1862.

Battles

Siege of Yorktown. April-May 1862.

Seven Days Battles. June 25-July 1, 1862.

First Manassas (Bull Run). Infantry and Cavalry. July 21, 1861.

Peninsular Campaign. All Elements. March-July 1862.

Seven Days Battles. All Elements. June 25-July 1, 1862.

Second Manassas (Bull Run). All Elements. August 28-30, 1862.

Sharpsburg (Antietam). Infantry. September 17, 1862.

Gettysburg. Cavalry and Artillery. July 1-3, 1863.

Wilderness. Primarily Infantry. May 5-7, 1864.

Siege of Petersburg. All Elements at Various Times. June 1864-March 1865.

Battle of Appomattox Court House. Infantry. April 9, 1865.

Battle of Bentonville. Cavalry and Artillery. March 19-21, 1865.

From *A Chronological History of the Hampton Legion Battalion of Cavalry* by Ron Crawley. [4]

Chapter 11

Killed in Action

In addition to her husband George, Great Grandmother Eleanor had three brothers in the war: First Lieutenant T.M. Boynton, Third Lieutenant M.M. Boynton, and Private Stephen D. Boynton. They were from Walterboro and were assigned to Company C, Beaufort District Troop, Hampton Legion, 3rd South Carolina Cavalry.

My Great Uncle Stephen Boynton was killed in action on May 5, 1862, during the Seige of Yorktown's Battle of Williamsburg, Virginia. He was buried in Cedar Grove Cemetery in old Williamsburg by his brother, 3rd Lt. Moses Boynton, Sergeant E. Prioleau Henderson from Walterboro, a very close friend of the Boynton family, and members of Company C.

The Civil War In My South

My Great Grand-Uncles
Private Stephen D. and Third Lieutenant Moses M. Boynton (with pistol)

Company A, Marion Men of Combahee, Hampton Legion, 3rd South Carolina Cavalry.

> *Sixth-plate ambrotype by an anonymous photographer. The Liljenquist Family Collection, Library of Congress.*

Henderson, as mentioned above, wrote a book in 1901 titled *Autobiography of Arab.* His memories of the war were written as his horse, Arab, would have seen it.

On page 84, he writes,

> *Here we found out the Beaufort District Troop had one man missing and the other companies several killed and wounded. The Beaufort Troop man was*

S.D. Boynton. My master volunteered to go with his brother and Nat Cannon and find him. We found him lying in the mud at the crossing, dangerously wounded under his sword arm, and in a dying condition. The men attempted to get him off, but he died before they got him to the top of the hill, trying to the last to utter some words to my master, who was supporting his head. Poor Steve Boynton. He was buried that night in old Williamsburg.

He sleeps his last sleep,

He has fought his last battle,

No sound can awaken him to glory again. [1]

Monument to Our Confederate Dead. [2]

The Williamsburg City Council removed this Confederate monument and published the following statement: Notice is hereby given that on July 14, 2020, the Williamsburg City Council voted to remove the monument to Confederate soldiers and sailors located in Bicentennial Park in the City of Williamsburg. Accessed August 10, 2021, https://www.williamsburg.gov/documentcenter/view/1238.

Cedar Grove Cemetery

Williamsburg, Virginia

Chapter 12

John Henry Patrick Belger

John Henry Patrick Belger was my maternal 2nd Great Grandfather. His parents were Henry Patrick Belger, 1800-, and Mary Fitzgerald Belger, 1812-abt 1859. He was born on April 21, 1832, in Hampton District. He died in 1880.

He had three brothers and two sisters: Edward Belger, 1834-1874; William Belger, 1837- ; John F. Belger, 1841- ; Julia Belger, 1841-1869; and Mary E. Belger, 1843-1885.

John married O. Elizabeth Hughes on May 22, 1855. They had eight children in 16 years: Julia Victoria Belger, 1856-1901; Mary Elizabeth Belger, Oct. 15, 1857-; John Miles Belger, 1858- ; William Belger, 1859- ; James Capers Belger, 1865-1929; Allen Johnson Belger, 1868-1938; Amy Ida Belger, 1869- ; and Joseph Ebinezal Belger, 1834-1874.

The 1850 U.S. Census indicates that John, age 13, lived with his mother and six siblings. There was no mention of his father. The 1860 Census shows John living in Prince William's Parish in Hampton County at Whippy Swamp. His occupation was "farmer."

Following his return from the war, the 1870 Census shows he was living in St. Peter's Parish at Hardeeville. Six children were still living with him and Elizabeth. His occupation had changed to "Stock Minder" and "Miller."

Concerning John's Confederate army service, he enlisted with the surname "Bulger." His family had emigrated from Ireland and did not change the name to Belger until later. On July 15, 1861, he was mustered in at Bay Point, Whippy Swamp, by Lt. H.S. Farley. He was a member of Company C, 11th Regiment, South Carolina Infantry.

Organized in the summer of 1861, the 11th Infantry Regiment was formed with men from Colleton, Clarendon, and Beaufort Counties. After serving in Charleston and fighting at Pocotaligo, the unit was sent to Hardeeville and assigned to Hagood's Brigade.

The unit was active in Charleston again during the summer of 1863. Later, it was assigned to Florida and then to Virginia in 1864. It fought in Drewry's Bluff, Cold Harbor, and Petersburg battles in Virginia. In 1865, the unit was on the move again. It was assigned to Fort Fisher in North Carolina, where it participated in the battle of Bentonville. This was the last battle of the war on the eastern seaboard.

On May 16, 1864, during the Bermuda Hundred Campaign in Bermuda Hundred, Virginia, John suffered a severe wound to his right arm from a minie ball. Bermuda Hundred was just outside Richmond, which was being threatened by Federal troops. After a series of battles, the Federals were stopped by Confederate forces under the command of General P.G.T. Beauregard.

John was taken to Jackson Hospital in Richmond, where his arm was amputated. He survived the war and received a certificate of disability when he was mustered out of the Confederate army.

South Carolina's 11th Infantry Regiment suffered the following casualties during the war.

Pocotaligo: Four killed. Fifteen wounded, Two missing.

Petersburg: Fourteen killed. Thirty-nine wounded. Twelve missing.

Deep Bottom: Fourteen killed. Twenty-eight wounded. Forty-five missing.

Weldon Railroad: The casualties amounted to almost 60% of the regiment.

When General Johnston surrendered to General Sherman at Bentonville on April 26, 1865, the South Carolina 11th Infantry Regiment had fewer men than an entire company.

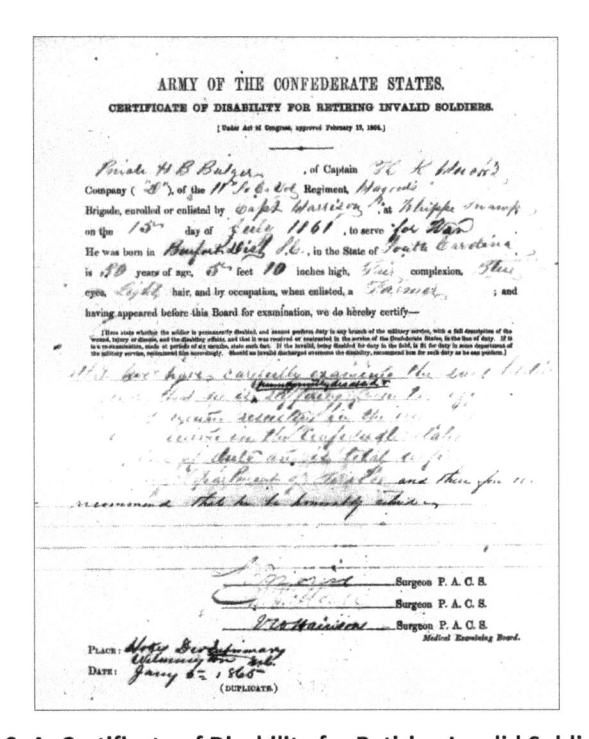

C. S. A. Certificate of Disability for Retiring Invalid Soldiers

"U.S. Civil War Soldiers, 1861-1865. National Park Service," Ancestry.com, Operations Inc., 2007, https://www.fold3.com.

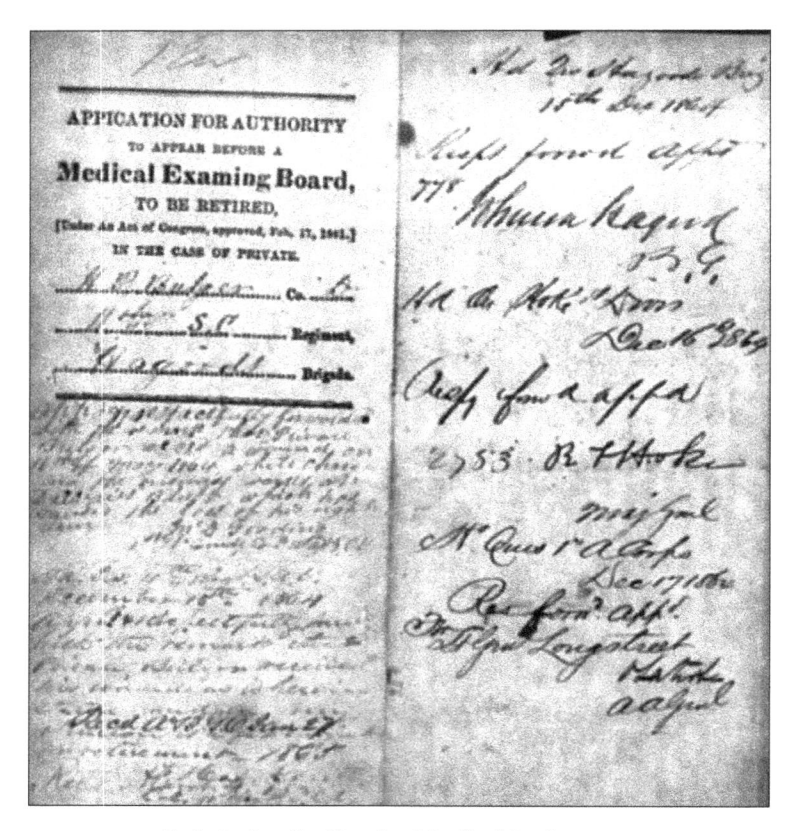

The Civil War In My South

C. S. A. Application for Medical Retirement

"U.S., Civil War Records and Profiles, 1861-1865," Ancestry.com, Operations Inc., 2009, https://www.fold3.com.

John Henry Patrick Belger

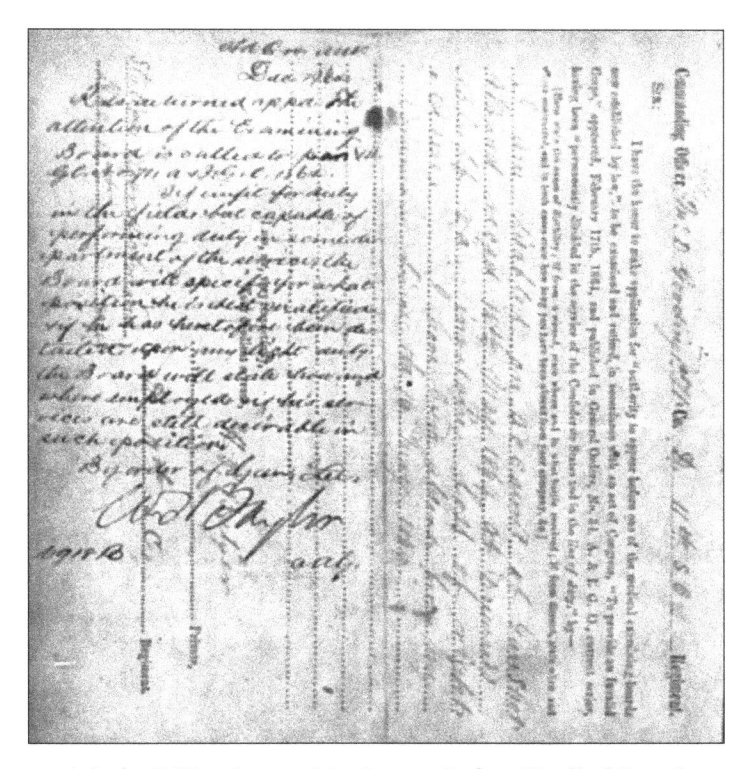

John's Written Request to Appear Before Medical Board

Retrieved February 14, 2021, http://www.fold3.com/image/259301462?xid=1945. Page 2-Civil War Soldiers-Confederate-Misc.

Retrieved February 14, 2021, http://www.fold3.com. Civil War Soldiers-Confederate-Misc at Fold3.

11th Regiment, South Carolina Infantry

Officers

Colonels: Daniel H. Ellis, F Hay Gantt, and William C. Heyward.
Lieutenant Colonels: Robert Campbell, Allen C. Izard, and William Shuler.
Majors: John J. Gooding, John H. Harrison, and B. Burgh Smith.

Assignments

Department of South Carolina, Georgia, and Florida. November 1861.

6th Military District. Department of South Carolina, Georgia, and Florida. December-June 1861.

4th Military District. Department of South Carolina, Georgia, and Florida. June-July 1862.

3rd Military District. Department of South Carolina, Georgia, and Florida. September 1862.

1st Sub-Division, 1st Military District. Department of South Carolina, Georgia, and Florida. July-August 1863.

Hagood's Brigade. 1st Sub-Division. 1st Military District. Department of South Carolina, Georgia, and Florida. September 1863.

Hagood's Brigade. Eastern Division. 7th Military District of South Carolina. Department of South Carolina, Georgia, and Florida. Except for Companies E and G assigned to the 3rd Military District of South Carolina. Department of South Carolina, Georgia, and Florida. October 1863.

2nd Military District of South Carolina. Department of South Carolina, Georgia, and Florida. December 1863.

Hagood's Brigade. 7th Military District of South Carolina. Department of South Carolina, Georgia, and Florida. January 1884.

District of Florida. Department of South Carolina, Georgia, and Florida. April 1864.

Hagood's Brigade. Hoke's Division. Department of North Carolina. May 1864.

Hagood's Brigade. Hoke's Division. 4th Corps. Army of Northern Virginia. Colonel Gantt was paroled and returned to resume command. October 1864.

Hagood's Brigade. Hoke's Division. Department of North Carolina. Lieutenant Colonel Izard resigned to return to the Navy. Major John J. Gooding took command of the regiment. December 1864.

Hagood's Brigade. Hoke's Division. Hardee's Corps. March 1865.

Hagood's Brigade. Hoke's Division. 1st Corps. Army of Tennessee. April 1865

Durham Station. Surrendered by General Johnston. April 26, 1865.

Battles

Port Royal. November 7, 1861.
Port Royal Ferry. June 6, 1862.
Port Royal Ferry. July 4, 1862.
Pinckney Island. August 21, 1862.
Coosawhatchie. October 22-23, 1862.
Destruction of the U.S. Army Steamer George Washington near Beaufort. April 9, 1863.
Pope's Island. May 19, 1863.
Combahee River. June 2, 1863.
Expedition from Fort Pulaski to Bluffton. June 4, 1863.

Expedition to Barnwell's Island. July 30, 1863.
Charleston Harbor. August-September 1863.
Swift Creek. May 9, 1864.
Drewry's Bluff. May 12, 1864.
Drewry's Bluff. May 16, 1864.
Cold Harbor. June 3, 1864.
Petersburg Siege. June 1864-April 1865.
Weldon Railroad. August 21, 1864.
2nd Fort Harrison. September 1864.
2nd Fort Harrison. January 13-15, 1865.
Carolinas Campaign. February-April, 1865.
Bentonville. March 19-21, 1865.

Roster

This regiment consisted of 2,432 men.

Company A. (Beaufort Volunteer Artillery). Mustered in on June 12, 1861, at Bay Point.

Company B. (St. Paul's Rifles). Mustered in on June 17, 1861.

Company C. (Summerville Rifles). Mustered in on July 6, 1861, at Hilton Head Island.

Company D. (Whippy Swamp Guards). Mustered in on July 15, 1861, at Bay Point.

Company E. (Hamilton Guards). Mustered in on June 23, 1861, at Bay Point.

Company F. (Republican Blues). Mustered in on August 5, 1861, at Braddocks Point.

Company G. (Butler Guards). Mustered in on August 29, 1861, at Otter Island.

Company H. (St. George Volunteers). Mustered in on July 26, 1861, at Hilton Head Island.

Company I.   (Colleton Guards).

Company K. (Round O Guards).

Source: *https://civilwarintheeast.com* [1]

Chapter 13

Uzziah Rentz

Uzziah Rentz was another maternal 2nd Great Grandfather. He was born in 1835 in Barnwell. His parents were Isaac and Keziah Kirkland Rentz. He died on March 11, 1906, in Hampton County at Varnville.

He had three brothers and one sister: Charles Rentz, 1830-April 15, 1864; Kesiah Rentz, 1844-?; Isaac Rentz, 1846-August 31, 1862; and Jacob Rentz, November 1, 1834-January 16, 1908.

The US 1860 Census indicates that Uzziah lived in Barnwell County at Buford Bridge. He was staying with John and Mary Craddock, ages 66 and 67. A young lady named Elizabeth Parker, age 22, also lived with the Craddock's.

When the war began, Uzziah enlisted in the 17th South Carolina Infantry at Camp Lee on January 2, 1862. He was assigned to Company G. Eight months later, during the Second Battle of Manassas (Bull Run) in Virginia, he suffered a severe would on August 31, 1862. As a result, the remainder of his service was spent in Confederate hospitals in Virginia, North Carolina, and Georgia.

On December 22, 1863, Uzziah appeared before a Medical Officer Examining Board at the Georgia Hospital in Augusta, Georgia. A partial transcript of their findings follows:

> *We certify that we have carefully examined Private Uzziah Rentz Co 'G' 17th SC regt and find him incapable of performing the duties of a soldier in the field, because of a gunshot wound of the lower third of the thigh received at the 2nd Battle of Manassas. The ball entered about three inches above the knee... It is extremely doubtful that the perfect use of the limb will be recovered.*
>
> *We therefore recommend he be detailed at 2nd Geo Hospital at Augusta Geo.*
>
> *Dec 22nd 1863* [1]

On December 29, 1863, General P.G.T. Beauregard approved the recommendation and ordered that Uzziah be detailed to serve as a hospital nurse.

The 17th Regiment had 304 men when they arrived for the Second Battle of Manassas. When it was over, the regiment had lost 186 casualties. Colonel Means was hit by a shell fragment and died the next day. Lieutenant Colonel McMaster was also wounded, but he was promoted to Colonel and took command of the regiment. Major John R. Culp, also injured, was promoted to lieutenant colonel, and Captain Sorrell was promoted to major.

DeWitt Boyd Stone, Jr. edited the book *Wandering To Glory*. It includes first-hand reports by some of the 17th Regiment's officers and men who fought at the Second Battle of Manassas. On page 54, Captain Edwards recorded,

The battle was opened about 4 P.M. by the Confederates advancing on Pope's lines. The fighting was fierce and continuous from about 4:30 until after sundown, when Pope's lines were all completely shattered and driven off the field. About 6 o'clock, Evans' Brigade was thrown against one of the strongest points in the Federal lines. It was on a hill covered with field batteries, supported by two heavy lines of infantry. They succeeded in breaking the Federal lines, but it was a fearful sacrifice. Colonels Means and Gadberry were both killed (Gadberry killed and Means mortally wounded).

In a number of the companies of the Seventeenth Regiment not an officer was left unhurt, and at least 75 percent of the men were either killed or wounded. More South Carolina blood was spilled in this battle than in any other battle of the war. [2]

In 1865, following the war, Uzziah married Sarah E. "Sallie" Chassereau from Bamberg in the old Barnwell District. They had eight children in 17 years: George Rentz, 1867-1931; Rosha Ann Rebecca Rentz, 1869-1914; Noah Rentz, 1871-1960; Carrie Rentz, 1873-1908; Franklin Rentz, 1877- ; Abijah Bijah Chassereau Rentz, 1878-1910; Barney Rasmer Rentz, 1882-1975; and Ann Rentz, 1884-1925.

In 1880, Uzziah, with his wife Sallie and six of their children, lived in Hampton County at Goethe, where he was a farmer. In 1890, he and Sallie were still farming. Their youngest son, Barnie, was the only child still living with them.

The Civil War In My South

Uzziah died on March 11, 1906, at Varnville, at 71. He was buried there at the old Rentz family farm cemetery.

Uzziah Rentz Grave Marker

Rentz Family Farm Cemetery
Varnville, South Carolina

Courtesy of Debbie Belger
Madison Heights, Michigan

Uzziah Rentz

CSA Casualty List Card.

Company Muster Roll. Oct. 1863. Absent. Wounded at 2nd Manassas, Ancestry.com, August 31, 1862, https://www.fold3.com.

The Civil War In My South

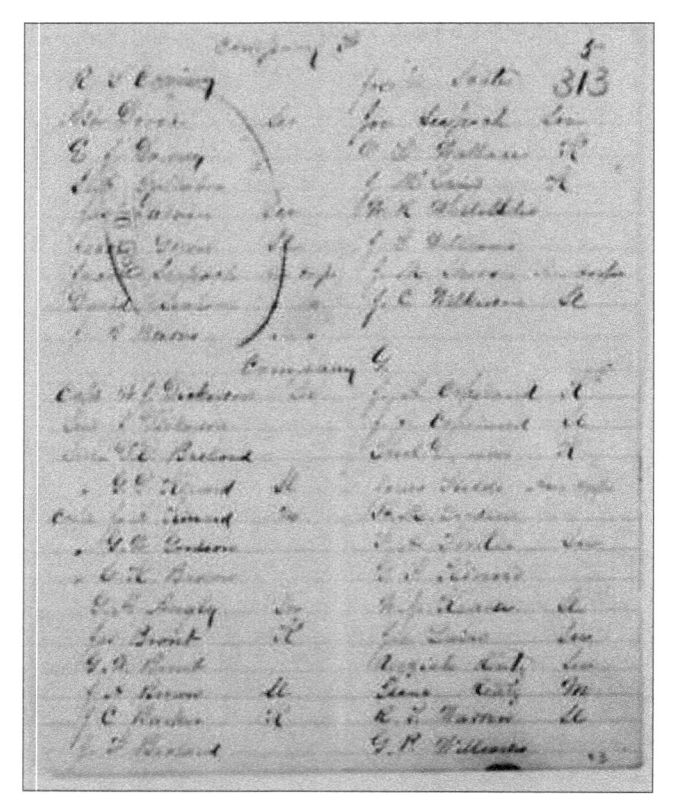

List of Casualties for Company G, 17th Infantry Regiment. SC Volunteers

Uzziah Rentz. "Casualty List for Wounded, Missing, or Killed for Company G, 17th Infantry Regiment, SC Volunteers.1862. Virginia and Maryland," Ancestry.com, retrieved May 21, 2015, https://www.fold3.com.

Fourth Name Up from Bottom Right

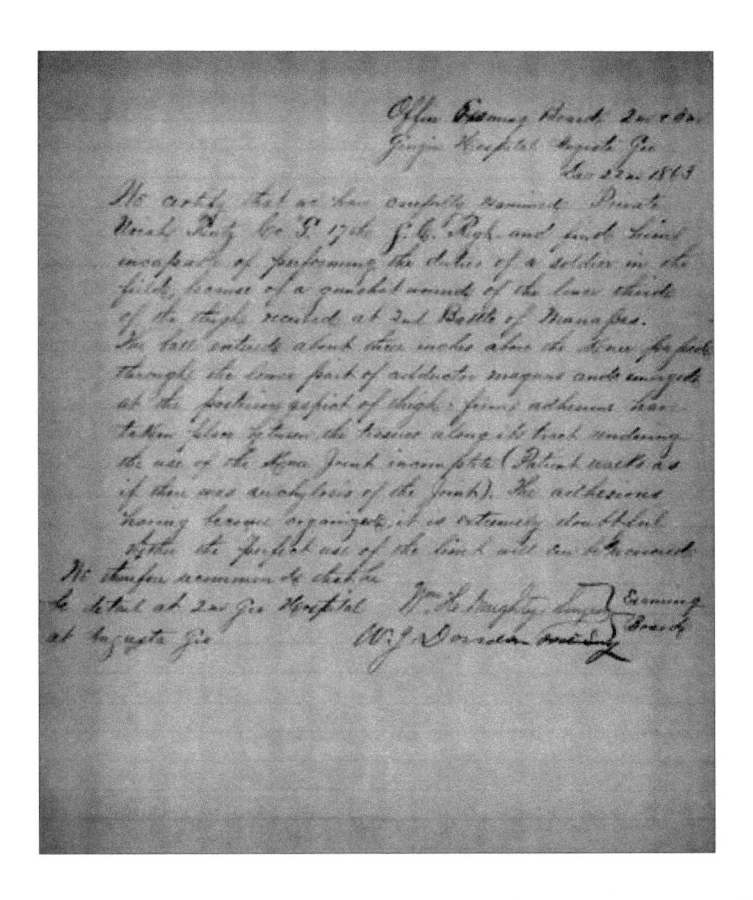

Hand-Written Report of Officer Examining Board. "Company Muster Roll for December 31, 1863. Detailed as Nurse," Ancestry.com, retrieved March 23, 2015, https://www.fold3.com.

The Civil War In My South

Company Muster Roll.

17th Regiment, South Carolina Infantry

Officers

Colonels: Fitz William McMaster and John H. Means.

Lieutenant Colonels: John R. Culp, Fitz William McMaster, and R.S. Means.

Majors: John W. Avery, Julius Mills, E.A. Crawford, John R. Culp, and R.S. Mean.

Assignments

3rd Military District of South Carolina. Department of South Carolina, Georgia, and Florida. Organized under the command of Colonel John H. Means, Lieutenant Colonel Fitz William McMaster, and Major R.S. Means. December 18, 1861.

2nd Military District of South Carolina. Department of South Carolina, Georgia, and Florida. June-July 1862.

Evan's Brigade. Drayton's Division. 1st Corps. Army of Northern Virginia. July 1862.

Evan's Independent Brigade, 1st Corps. Army of Northern Virginia. August-October 1862.

Evan's Brigade. McLaw's Division. 1st Corps. Army of Northern Virginia. October-November 1862.

Evan's Brigade. French's Command. Department of North Carolina and Southern Virginia. November-February 1862.

Evan's Brigade. District of Cape Fear. Department of North Carolina and Southern Virginia. February-March 1863.

Evan's Brigade. 1st Military District of South Carolina. Department of South Carolina, Georgia, and Florida. May 1863.

Evan's Brigade. French's Division. Department of the West. June-July 1863.

Evan's Brigade. French's Division. Department of Mississippi and East Louisiana. July-August 1863.

Evan's Brigade. 2nd Sub-Division. 1st Military District of South Carolina. Department of South Carolina, Georgia, and Florida. August-September 1863.

Eastern Division. 7th Military District of South Carolina. Department of South Carolina, Georgia, and Florida. October-November 1863.

Elliott's Brigade. 1st Military District of South Carolina. Department of South Carolina, Georgia, and Florida. December 1863.

Elliott's-Wallace's Brigade. Johnston's Division. Department of North Carolina and Southern Virginia. June 1864.

Appomattox Court House. The regiment surrendered nine officers and 110 men. April 9, 1865.

Battles

2nd Manassas. August 28-30, 1862
South Mountain. September 14, 1862
Sharpsburg. September 17, 1862

Kinston. December 31, 1862
Jackson. May 14, 1863
Bermuda Hundred. May 17-June, 1864
Petersburg. June 1864
Petersburg. Battle of the Crater. July 30, 1864
Fort Steadman. March 25, 1865
Five Forks. April 1, 1865
Appomattox. April 9, 1865

Roster

This regiment contained 2,074 men.

Company A. (Richland/Chester)
Company B. (Fairfield Lyle's Rifles)
Company C. (York Broad River Light Infantry)
Company D. (Chester)
Company E. (Fort Mill/York Indian Land Tigers)
Company F. (York Carolina Rifles)
Company G. (Barnwell)
Company H. (Barnwell)
Company I. (Lancaster/York/Spartanburg Lancaster Tigers)
CompaNY k. (York Lacy Guards)

Source: Steve A. Hawks. *Confederate Armies and Departments in the Eastern Theater. 17th Regiment, South Carolina Infantry.* Retrieved September 18, 2021. https://civilwarintheeast.com. [3]

Isaac J. Rentz

Uzziah's brother, Isaac J. Rentz, also enlisted and joined Company G. At 17, Isaac was mustered in at Camp Lee by Captain Kearse on

January 3, 1862. He died at Second Manassas in the same battle on the same day Uzziah was wounded, August 31, 1862,

In a statement dated November 4, 1863, Lieutenant J.H. Kearse, Commander of Company G., wrote,

> I certify that the within named Isaac Rentz, a private of Capt. Dickinson's Co. G. of the 17th Regt. South Carolina Volunteers, born in Barnwell District, in the state of South Carolina, aged 17 years, 5 feet 6 inches high, fair complexion, blue eyes and by occupation a farmer, was enlisted by Capt. Kearse at Camp Lee on the 3rd day of January, 1862, to serve one year. He died on the 31st August 1862, from wound received at the battle of Manassas, Va, on the previous day.
>
> The said Isaac Rentz was last paid by Maj. Bryan to include the 30th day of April 1862, and has pay due him for that time to the day of his death.
>
> There is due him forty-four Dollars.
>
> J.H. Kearse
> Lieut Comdg
> Co. G.
> 17th Regt. SCV.
>
> Source: Fold3.com [4]

Charles Rentz

Charles Rentz, another brother, was born in Barnwell County in 1830. He married Eve Chassereau, also from Barnwell County. They had three children. The U.S. 1860 Census recorded them as living at Cowpen Branch, in Barnwell District. At some point, Charles moved his family to Lake City, Florida.

Charles joined the CSA on November 7, 1862, at Barnwell. He was mustered in as a Private with Company L, 11th Regiment, South Carolina Reserves. [5] Following his service, Charles returned to Lake City, where he remained until his death on April 15, 1864.

Jacob Rentz

In Barnwell, Jacob Rentz, Uzziah's second oldest brother, was born on November 1, 1834. He enlisted in the South Carolina 11th Infantry, 9th Volunteers, at Colleton (Walterboro) on March 20, 1862.

Following the war, Jacob married Matilda Catherine Kinard in 1868. They had three children together. Matilda died in 1883. Later that year, Jacob married Hannah Mary Rentz. He had five additional children with Hannah. Hannah died in 1891, leaving Jacob as a widower for the second time.

Jacob died at the age of 73 on January 16, 1908. He was buried in the Folk Cemetery in Bamberg County.

Chapter 14

Noah Cleland

Noah Cleland was also my maternal 2nd Great Grandfather. He was born in 1835 in Ridgeland. His parents were John and Mary Holland Cleland. John, 1747-1833, and Mary, 1796-1880. They were married on April 25, 1810, in Charleston. Mary was 14 years old. [1]

In 1850, Noah was 16 years old. He lived in Prince William's Parish at Beaufort with his mother and three of his siblings: Robert Cleland, Barnwell Cleland, and Edwin Cleland. [2]

Noah married Elizabeth Anne Stanley, 1796-1880, on January 1, 1857, in Beaufort. In 1860, the US Census listed their residence as St. Luke's Parish at Gillisonville. He and Elizabeth had their first two children with them: Elias Cleland, 1858-?; and John Cleland, 1861-1935. Noah's occupation was listed as "Farmer." [3]

Noah enlisted in Company C, 3rd Cavalry Regiment, South Carolina Volunteers, when the Civil War started. He was mustered in at Grahamville on March 27, 1862. He likely knew my Great Grandfather George since they served in the same regiment. [4]

The Civil War In My South

Noah returned to Gillisonville after the war ended in 1865. The 1870 census reveals that he resumed farming and having children. Added to the list were: Elias, 12; John, 9; Frances (my great grandmother), 7; Mary, 5; Alice, 4; June, 2; and Elmore, two months. [5]

By 1880, the Census indicated that Noah and his family had moved about six miles east to Coosawhatchie. He was still farming, and his family had continued to grow. Joining him and Elizabeth were their children: John, now 22; Frank, 19; Mary, 16; Alice, 14; Ulmer, 12; Hans, 6; Benny, 4; Ella, 3; and George, 1. [6]

At 82, Elizabeth died in Ridgeland on January 17, 1922. She was buried at the Oak Grove Baptist Church Cemetery in Grays. Noah died on August 3, 1935, at the age of 100. He was buried beside his wife.

Grave Marker for Noah and Elizabeth Cleland

Oak Grove Baptist Church Cemetery
Grays, South Carolina

Courtesy of Debbie Belger
Madison Heights, Michigan

Chapter 15

Sherman's War on Civilians

After Maj. General William T. Sherman captured Savannah, Georgia, Lt. General Grant ordered him to proceed to Virginia. Grant knew South Carolina was no longer a threat to the Union, and he wanted Sherman's army to assist in the fight against General Lee.

But, Sherman had other plans for South Carolina that did not involve winning the war. Shortly before he invaded the State's Lowcountry, Sherman wrote a letter to General Henry Halleck, his commanding officer. He informed Halleck, "We are not only fighting hostile armies, but a hostile people, and must make old and young, rich and poor, feel the hard hand of war…The truth is the whole army is burning with an insatiable desire to wreak vengeance upon South Carolina." On December 13, 1864, Sherman again made it clear to Halleck, "The whole army is crazy to be turned loose in Carolina," [1]

Some might think Sherman's desire for retribution was based on South Carolina having more slaves than any other Confederate state. That is an incorrect assumption. Writing to Maj. R.M. Sawyer, on January 31, 1864, Sherman stated the war was the result of a "false political doctrine that any and all people have a right to self-government." That same letter was published in *The Rebellion Record* in 1865. After asserting the Federal government's right to take the property and lives of anyone who refused to submit to its authority, Sherman stated the "political nonsense of slave rights, State rights, freedom of conscience, freedom of press, and other such trash" had "deluded the Southern people into war." [2]

One of Sherman's aides, Major George W. Nichols, wrote a book in 1865 about the South Carolina campaign. He described his contempt for the people stating they were "the scum, the lower dregs of civilization. They are not Americans; they are merely South Carolinians." [3]

General Hugh Judson Kilpatrick commanded Sherman's cavalry. He and his troops entered Barnwell in February 1865. Willian Gilmore Simms, a well known South Carolina author, described what he saw,

> *We had no army there for its defense; no issue of strength. Yet it was plundered-every house-and nearly all burned to the ground, and this, too, where the town was occupied by women and children only. So, too, the fate of Blackville, Graham, Bamberg, Buford's Bridge, Lexington, etc., all hamlets of most modest character, where no resistance was offered-where no fighting took place-where there was no provocation of liquor even, and where the only exercise of heroism was at the expense of women, infancy, and feebleness.* [4]

In his autobiography, General Oliver Otis Howard wrote about a conversation he had with Sherman. Sherman told him, *I sent Kilpatrick to Barnwell, and he changed the name to Burnwell.* Howard later told Kilpatrick about Sherman's joke and said they found it very amusing. [5]

Simms further wrote,

> *The inhabitants, black no less than white were left to starve, compelled to feed only upon the garbage to be found in the abandoned camps of the soldiers. The corn scraped up from the spots where the horses fed, has been the only means of life left to thousands.*
>
> *And through plundering, and burning, the troops made their way through a portion of Beaufort into Barnwell District, where they pursued the same game. The village of Buford's Bridge, of Barnwell, Blackville, Graham's, Bamberg, Midway, were more or less destroyed; the inhabitants everywhere left homeless and without food. The horses and mules, all cattle and hogs, whenever fit for service or food, were carried off, and the rest shot. Every implement of the workman or the farmer, tools, plows, hoes, gins, looms, wagons,vehicles, was made to feel the flames. From Barnwell to Orangeburg and Lexington was the next progress, marked everywhere by the same sweeping destruction.* [6]

Sherman also exhibited racism toward all African Americans. Michael Fellman, Sherman's biographer, stated, *They were a less-than-human and savage race, uncivilized to white standards, and probably un-civilizable. They were obstacles to the upward sweep of history, progress, wealth, and white destiny.* [7]

Thomas G. Robisch, writing in the *Emory International Law Review,* said, Sherman's *treatment of runaway slaves was so wretched that, despite the fact that his army overflowed with foodstuffs and supplies, any civilians unlucky enough to be caught in his army's rapaciously destructive path, soon found he failed to leave behind any food, medicine, and shelter to meet their human needs.* [8]

On July 31, 1862, Sherman wrote a letter to his wife in which he said his goal during the war was *the extermination, not of soldiers alone, that is the least part of the trouble, but the [Southern] people.* His wife replied that her fondest wish was for a war of *extermination and that all [Southerns] would be driven like the swine into the sea.* [9]

Historian Jacqueline G. Cambell wrote about the treatment of African American women by the Federal soldiers. She stated they considered the women as *legitimate prey of lust.* She further described an eyewitness report of a lady in Summerton who said she *saw the soldiers go after young black women every night. The girls had to hide in the woods to save themselves from being ravished.* [10]

Toward the end of Thomas Osborn's book, he wrote in March 1865,

> *The suffering which the people will have to undergo will be most intense. We have left on the wide strip of country we have passed over no provisions which will go any distance in supporting the people. We have left no stock by means of which they can get more. All horses, mules and cattle, sheep and hogs*

> have been taken. They cannot go outside of the country traversed for lack of transportation...Even before we came into the State the provisions were vastly greater than we had supposed. We have been out on this trip a little longer than before, and made the same distance, and covered the same or a greater breadth of territory, and have again left nothing. I do not think that the Rebel armies will not fight, they will do so whenever an opportunity offers, which affords a hope of success. They still believe their government, their property, their honor, and their Southern pride is at stake, and they will fight for them. [11]

All the plantations in my Lowcountry which were in Sherman's path were burned and destroyed. This included anything and everything the Federal troops could not use. A large number of them were located in Coosawhatchie's surrounding area.

Roseland Plantation, on the Coosawhatchie River, was no exception. David Huguenin initially bought the property after being confiscated from a Tory baron in 1782. At the start of the Civil War, Roseland comprised 25,000 acres, including three antebellum houses. Sherman's troops burned everything.

Interestingly, a Federal officer in charge of the burning was Leonard H. Huguenin. While going through some papers in one of the houses, he discovered he was related to the owner. Seven years later, William T. Colcock, Jr., Col. Colcock's brother, received a letter from Edgar Daniel Huguenin. My friend Julius Huguenin, a fellow native of Coosawhatchie, grew up at Roseland with his siblings. They are direct descendants of David Huguenin. Julius gave me a copy of the letter. The latter part states,

> *I could have written to some of you long ago as I have a paper in my possession taken from your grandfather's house by my brother during the war. He was an officer in the 1444th N.Y. Volunteers, when stationed at Folly Island they made a raid up the Pocotaligo river. Of course they destroyed all that came in their way, and while in your Grandfather's house learned by the papers he found there that it belonged to a person whose name was the same as his own, and whose family was the same as that of which he was a branch; I hope you will do him justice in believing that he did all in his power to prevent the destruction of the property. The papers are valuable only as curiosities. …If you have any questions to ask, I will be pleased to answer them if I can and hope you will favor me with your family tree, root and branch. Yours very truly, E. D. Huguenin. 78 Franklin St. N.Y.*

Roseland is still owned by the well-known and respected Huguenin family. Only the avenue of oaks and the family cemetery remain. My family owned the adjoining property at Bee's Creek in the early 1900s. My mother was born there in 1911.

The North viewed Sherman as a hero. Perhaps many still do. The South considered him to be a villain with no redeeming qualities. Most of us born and bred in South Carolina still feel that way. While I make no excuses for any dishonorable conduct by Confederate soldiers, any such behavior pales in comparison to Sherman's and his soldiers' actions during their march through the Palmetto State.

Chapter 16

Charles Jones Colcock

Col. Charles Jones Colcock was born on April 30, 1820, about ten miles south of Barnwell at Boiling Springs. His parents were Thomas H. Colcock and Mary Eliza Hay of the old Beaufort District. Col. Colcock was named for his grandfather, Judge Charles Jones Colcock, with whom he lived for much of his childhood.

Charles married Caroline Heyward in 1838. She was the granddaughter of Thomas Heyward, one of South Carolina's signers of the Declaration of Independence, buried at his plantation in Old House close to Grahamville. Charles and Caroline lived on his plantation on the Okatie River near Bluffton. They had two children together.

He later bought another plantation near Port Royal and planted sea island cotton. Charles was not college-educated like most of his peers, but he was an intelligent, refined gentleman who was well respected. He recognized that if his cotton venture proved successful, a railroad would be needed for additional means of transporting his crops. He proposed this to a group of his wealthy colleagues, and the Charleston Savannah Railroad was built. That railroad would later become very important to the Confederacy's ability to protect the Lowcountry, and it would also become a primary target of the Federal army.

In 1851, Charles married Lucy Frances Horton. He had three additional children with her. Lucy died of pneumonia before Charles joined the Confederate States Army.

He was born and lived all of his life in my South Carolina Lowcountry. He had no military experience, but he was a gifted horseman and businessman. He was also very well known throughout the region and was elected colonel of the South Carolina 3rd Cavalry Regiment in 1862. He commanded about 1,000 men from Beaufort, Barnwell, Colleton, and Charleston Districts. Great Grandfather George was one of them, and he served with Col. Colcock for the duration of the war.

Honey Hill is perhaps the best known of all the 3rd Cavalry's battles in my South Carolina Lowcountry. It is the subject of Chapter Eight of this book. The battle was fought to defend the same railroad which Charles had played a significant role in constructing. This was the fourth and final battle guarding the railroad. All of them were Confederate victories against overwhelming numbers of Federal troops.

An interesting side note is that before arriving at Honey Hill, Charles rode by his fiance's house to tell her their wedding, planned for the same day as the battle, had to be postponed for three days. The following month in December, he and Agnes Bostick were married. They had four children. After the war, they spent most of their life together in Barnwell.

Charles Jones Colcock

Major General Gustavus W. Smith brought his small Georgia infantry to Honey Hill. He was the senior officer there, but he soon relinquished his full command to Colonel Colcock. Smith recognized his limitations in not knowing anything about the area. His wisdom and humility were fortunate that day for the Confederate forces.

Captain William A. Courtenay was present at the battle. He was serving as a special correspondent for the *Charleston Mercury* newspaper. The day after the battle, Courtenay interviewed General Smith. He congratulated him on his quick arrival with his troops. The general pointed to Colonel Colcock and stated, "Captain! Congratulate that gentleman; he was the active commander on the field, placed all the troops and is entitled to the honors he has won," [1] Courtenay would later write what he called a memoir of Colcock. It would be published in the *Charleston Mercury* and the *Southern Historical Society Papers: Volume 26*.

Included in his memoir was this tribute by Rev. John G. Williams, who served as Chaplain for the 3rd Cavalry from its organization until its surrender,

> *I was near Colonel Colcock those four years in camp, on the march, in battle, and can truly say South Carolina sent to the war no son nobler, braver, more devoted to the cause, than Charles Jones Colcock. A typical gentleman, he stood before his regiment, numbering over one thousand men, an inspiring example, to be honored and imitated. Nothing mean came near his head or heart. He was a sincere Christian; his life in the army contradicted the general belief that it was impossible to lead a Christian life in camp; he was the same there as*

at home. No one ever heard an oath or improper story from his lips.; he felt the responsibility of his position, and did his duty daily to his command, his country, and his God.

I can never forget the disbanding of the regiment at Union Court House. After telling the several companies that the war was over, and bidding each and all an affectionate farewell, he retired to his tent, and, unable to restrain his feelings, sobbed aloud with uncontrollable grief.

His death was a very happy one. While passing through the valley of the shadow of death he asked his wife to sing his favorite hymn, 'Jesus, Lover of My Soul,' which she tried to do, and weak as he was he tried to join. In the fight with the enemies of his country he was vanquished; in his last fight with death he was more than conqueror, through the Great Captain of his salvation, whom he loved and trusted. [2]

Col. Colcock died on October 22, 1891. He was buried at Stoney Creek Cemetery in Sheldon.

Col. Charles Jones Colcock's Grave Marker

Stoney Creek Cemetery
Sheldon, South Carolina

Courtesy of Larry DuBose
Ridgeland, South Carolina

Chapter 17

Robert E. Lee

Robert Edward Lee was born on January 19, 1807, in Stratford Hall, Virginia. On October 12, 1870, he died in Lexington, Virginia. He was buried at University Chapel, Washington and Lee University.

Much has been written about Lee's life and his service to the United States and later the Confederate States of America. Revered in the south during the war, he became even more revered after his surrender. Stonewall Jackson had been the great Confederate hero for much of the war. Toward the end of the 19th century, Lee was even admired by many in the North based on his character and his devotion to duty.

Benjamin Harvey Hill was a politician who opposed secession but stayed with the South. He served as a Confederate senator representing Georgia. In 1874, he addressed the Southern Historical Society in Atlanta and said this about Lee:

He was a foe without hate; a friend without treachery; a soldier without cruelty; a victor without oppression, and a victim without murmuring. He was a public officer without vices; a private citizen without wrong; a neighbour without reproach; a Christian without hypocrisy, and a man without guile. He was a Caesar, without his ambition; Frederick, without his tyranny; Napoleon, without his selfishness, and Washington, without his reward. [1]

In the Introduction of his book, *Lee in the Lowcountry,* Daniel J. Crooks, Jr, writes,

> *The historian Bruce Catton once said of Robert E. Lee's early career: 'If he had disappeared from view at the end of 1861, he would figure in today's footnotes as a promising officer, who somehow did not live up to expectations.' In 1861, Lee was a man rooted in reality. All around him, Lee saw the lack of resources needed to make war. Far from conceding a contest that was ordained to fail, Lee forged ahead with a resolve to get Virginia and the Confederacy ready to meet the Federal onslaught. Lee oversaw the recruits as they were mustered, equipped and drilled. The Rebel army that fought at Bull Run was the product of organizational genius.* [2]

Lee had gone to Richmond in late April 1861 to take command of Virginia's military forces at the invitation of Gov. John Letcher. When the militias and volunteer armies of other states who joined the Confederacy were under the command of the Provisional Confederate Army, Lee took on the critical task of molding the various locally formed units into a unified fighting force.

In the fall of 1861, Confederate President Jefferson Davis sent Lee to western Virginia to resolve a disagreement between two generals who were focused on their careers instead of leading the

Robert E. Lee

Confederacy to victory. Their commanding officer was unable to correct the stalemate. Lee did bring the forces together, but that did not result in a victory at Cheat Mountain. Lee returned to Richmond and took responsibility for the failure. Davis, however, knew the real story. He did not lose faith in Lee's ability.

The Federal navy had already begun a blockade of the South in July 1861, and by November 7, they had taken Fort Beauregard and Fort Walker. These victories led to the fall of Port Royal Island and then the occupation of the Sea Islands along South Carolina's coast. Governor F. W. Pickens was particularly invested in equipping and deploying South Carolina troops. He had begun to raise an infantry regiment before the firing on Fort Sumter, believing correctly that the north would not quickly abandon the forts on Charleston harbor. After the war began in earnest, he continued to work vigorously for South Carolina's defense.

Battle of Port Royal

Courtesy of the Jasper County Historical Society
Ridgeland, South Carolina

Following the capture of Hilton Head, Beaufort, and other sea islands by the Federal troops, Lee received command of the coastal military department of South Carolina, Georgia, and East Florida. He established his headquarters in Coosawhatchie, where he proceeded to plan the strategy and defenses to contain the enemy.

Lee wrote to Governor Pickens on December 27, 1861,

> *I have had the honor to receive your letter of the 20th inst: In a previous letter I endeavored to express to your Excell'cy, my entire willingness to arm certain companies of regiments already in the service named by you, provided any arms remained after arming the regiments being organized for the war. But I cannot issue to them arms, before the arming of the regiments is completed.*
>
> *If the companies of Capn Blains, McCord & Rims, which I understand are for the war and attached by you to Steven's Legion, were assigned to the Batt. Commanded by Lieut Col Moore which embraces the six companies attached to Orr's reg't, this Battn. Wd. Only require one company for the formation of a reg't & might then be armed with the Enfield Rifle. My object is to make the arms available for the defence of the State, as soon as possible and I hope your Excell'cy will aid me in this.*
>
> *Major James battn. has been ordered to report to Genl. Evans, who is in great need of troops. Genl. Ripley informs me that Cols Elford & Means reg'ts will not be able to take the field for some days. In*

Robert E. Lee

the meantime he has sent forward Col. Steven's legion to reinforce Gen. Evans.

The enemy is making demonstrations ag'st Wadmalaw Is'd, and our force there is not strong enough to resist him.

Since your letter authorizing me to take command of the State Troops in the field, I have felt no hesitation in doing so. Previously although aware that certain forces were called into service and placed under the command of Gen Ripley, I did not know where or how it was designed to use them. According to the last returns received, the number of troops mustered in Confed. Service from So. Carolina, within the Dept:, present for duty, is 10,036, including Offrs., Non Comd. Offs. & P'vts.

The strength of the 4h. Brigade S.C. Militia (D Saussures), present for duty, inclu'dg Offs., non:comd. Offs. & pv'ts is reported to be 1,531. Its total strength present and absent is 2,021, and differs from the number stated in your Excellency's letter, which is 3,420.

The strength of the 4h. Brigade S.C. Militia (D Saussures), present for duty, inclu'dg Offs., non:comd. Offs. & pv'ts is reported to be 1.531. Its total strength present and absent is 2.021, and differs from the number stated in your Excellency's letter, which is 3.420.

The strength of Col. Martin's regiment in the field, by the last returns, is 628. The number reported for duty including Offs. non: comd. Offs. & pvts is 567. The number of troops in Confed. States service, as stated above (10,036), does not include the reg'ts of Col's Elford & Means, the Laurens Battn. & the other companies mentioned in your letter, which have arrived since the Return's were made. In addition to this force, there are two reg'ts from No. Ca. , two from Tenne., one from Virg'a and four field Batteries. My object is to inform your Ex'cy of the amount of the force for actual service in the State. You must however bear in mind that the garrisons for the forts at Georgetown, of Ft. Moultrie, Fts. Sumter, Johnson, Castle Pinckney & the field works for the defence of the approaches through Stono, Wappo & which embrace the best and steadiest of our troops, cannot be removed from their posts and must not therefore be included in the force for operations in the field. The strength of the enemy, as far as I am able to judge, exceeds the whole force that we have in the State; it can be thrown with great celerity against any point, and far outnumbers any force we can bring against it in the field.

I am with the highest esteem / Your obt. servant R E Lee / Genl. Comdg [3]

Gov'r to Genl Lee / about So Ca Troops / Dec'r 27th 1861.

Genl. Gist will - see that Genl. Lee puts the force from this Ste into Confederate service at 10,036 -- does this include the garrisons at the forts or not - does it include Manigault's rgts at Georgetown

> *of 12 companies 1148 -men. Please make the true state of things appear.*
>
> *The return of DeSaussure's Brigade was last number 3,400 & this included all - I only meant as its number, but I knew only about 1600 were ever out.*
>
> *F W Pickens / 29. Decr. 1861 Let me know & Moses will copy for to be sent into the Convention. F W P* [4]

Crooks continued in his book to describe Lee's difficult task, "Beyond the need to build forts and earthworks, Lee had to organize the chaos of state volunteers, state politicians and the constant reality of the South's martial resources. By early 1862, Lee was overwhelmed by the need to do so much with so little. Command of an actual army eluded Lee; instead, he remained at the disposal of President Davis." [5]

Even with all the difficulties facing him during his assignment at Coosawhatchie, history confirms that Lee could still lead with confidence and inspire those under his command.

To Lee's credit, his planning, organization, and fortifications during his brief time at Coosawhatchie prevented the railroad's destruction. The Federals tried four times to do so but were defeated each time by the Confederates. It was not until Sherman's troops arrived in 1865 that the railroad was finally destroyed along with everything else.

Chapter 18

Traveller

There are different accounts of how Lee obtained his favorite and famous war horse. We do know he took possession of Traveller during his assignment at Coosawhatchie. The following is a narrative from the previous owner.

> *Traveller was raised by Mr. Johnston, near the Blue Sulphur Springs, in Greenbrier County, Va; was of the "Gray Eagle" stock...when the Wise Legion was encamped on Sewell Mountains, opposing the advance of the Federal army under Rosecrans, in the fall of 1861, I was major of the Third Regiment of Infantry in that legion, and my brother Capt. Joseph M. Brown, was quartermaster...I authorized my brother to purchase a good, serviceable horse of the best Greenbrier stock for our use during the war...he came across the horse above mentioned, and I purchased him for $175 (gold value) in the fall of 1861, of Capt. J.W. Johnston, son of the Mr. Johnson first above mentioned.*
>
> *When Gen. Lee took command of the Wise Legion and the Floyd Brigade...in the fall of 1861, he first*

saw this horse, and took a great fancy to it. He called it his colt, and said he would need it before the war was over. Whenever the General saw my brother he had something pleasant to say to him about "my colt" as he designated him.

The Third Regiment was...ordered to the South Carolina coast...upon seeing my brother on this horse near Pocotaligo...Gen. Lee at once recognized the horse...my brother then offered him the horse as a gift, which the General promptly declined, and at the same time remarked: "If you willingly sell me the horse, I will gladly use it for a week or so, to learn its qualities." Thereupon my brother had the horse sent to Gen. Lee's stable.

In about a month the horse was returned to my brother, with a note from Gen. Lee stating that the animal suited him, but that he could no longer use so valuable a horse in such times unless it were his own... this was in February 1862...my brother wrote me of Lee's desire to have the horse, and asked me what to do. I replied at once "if he will not keep it then sell it to him at what it cost me." He sold the horsr to Gen. Lee for $200 in currency, the $25 having been added by Gen. Lee to the price for the horse in September, 1861, to make up for depreciation in our currency from Sptember to February, 1862.

Thomas L. Brown, August 10, 1886 [1]

After taking possession of his prized warhorse, Lee decided to spell Traveller with two Ls. Included in the *Riding Aside* Blogspot on April 29, 2011, was this post-war description of Taveller,

After the war, Traveller accompanied Lee to Washington College in Lexington, Virginia. He lost many hairs from his tail to admirers (veterans and college students) who wanted a souvenir of the famous horse and his general. Lee wrote to his daughter Mildred that 'The boys are plucking out his tail, and he is presenting the appearance of a plucked chicken.' In 1870, during Lee's funeral procession, Traveller was led behind the caisson bearing the General's casket, his saddle and bridle draped with black crepe. Not long after Lee's death, in 1871, Traveller stepped on a nail and developed tetanus. There was no cure, and he was euthanized to relieve his suffering.

Robert E. Lee and the Mist of the Coosawhatchie.

A high school classmate took this picture of the print and gave it to me. He found the print at a garage sale many years ago and bought it because the title included Coosawhatchie. The drawing consists of Lee on Traveller, in the shallows of the Coosawhatchie River in Coosawhatchie, SC. Lee looks toward the First Baptist Church at Coosawhatchie, established in 1759. This is the only image of the original church I have been able to find.

Courtesy of Mike Thomas
Okatie, South carolina

Traveller was initially buried behind the main buildings of the college, but was unearthed by persons unknown and his bones were bleached for exhibition in Rochester, New York, in 1875/1876. In 1907, Richmond journalist Joseph Bryan paid to have the bones mounted and returned to the college, named Washington and Lee University since Lee's death, and they were displayed in the Brooks Museum, in what is now Robinson Hall. The skeleton was periodically vandalized there by students who carved their initials in it for good luck. In 1929, the bones were moved to the museum in the basement of the Lee Chapel, where they stood for 30 years, deteriorating with exposure.

Finally in 1971, Traveller's remains were buried in a wooden box encased IN CONCRETE NEXT TO THE Lee Chapel on the Washington & Lee campus, a few feet away from the Lee family crypt inside, where his master's body rests. The stable where he lived his last days, directly connected to the Lee House on campus, traditionally stands with its doors left open; this is said to allow his spirit to wander freely. The 24th President of Washington & Lee (and thus a recent resident of Lee House), Dr. Thomas Burish, caught strong criticism from many members of the Washington & Lee community for closing the stable gates in violation of this tradition. Burish later had the doors to the stable repainted in a dark green color, which he referred to in campus newspapers as 'Traveller Green.'

The base newspaper of the United States Army's Fort Lee, located in Petersburg, Virginia, is named Traveller.

Traveller remains in the hearts and minds of Washington and Lee students to this day, and is the namesake of the University's Safe Ride Program. Students are known to exclaim 'Call Traveller and you will get home safely'. [3]

Traveller's Grave Site at Washington and Lee University.

"Traveller (Horse). Death and Burials," Wikiwand, retrieved August 23, 2021, https://www.wikiwand.com/en/Traveller_(horse).

The Civil War In My South

"General Lee on His Beloved Traveller,"

Retrieved August 23, 2021

https://www.wikiwand.com/en/Traveller_(horse)#/overview.

Chapter 19

Lee's Letters to His Family from Coosawhatchie

Robert E. Lee Jr., the third son and sixth child of Robert E. and Mary Lee, graduated from the University of Virginia and served as an aide to his brother Custis. In 1904, Robert published his *Recollections and Letters of General Lee,* an account of his father's memories and the daily life at Arlington house.

General Lee wrote the following letters during his service at Coosawhatchie. They are personal and give insight into his thoughts during a most challenging assignment.

To his wife, Mary:

From Savannah, November 18, 1861.

> *My Dear Mary: This is the first moment I have had to write to you, and now am waiting the call to breakfast, on my way to Brunswick, Fernandina, etc. This is my second visit to Savannah. Night before last, I returned to Coosawhatchie, South Carolina,*

> from Charleston, where I have placed my headquarters, and last night came here, arriving after midnight. I received in Charleston your letter from Shirley. It was a grievous disappointment to me not to have seen you, but better times will come, I hope.... You probably have seen the operations of the enemy's fleet. Since their first attack they have been quiescent apparently, confining themselves to Hilton Head, where they are apparently fortifying.
>
> I have no time for more. Love to all.
>
> Yours very affectionately and truly,
>
> R. E. Lee.

To his wife:

From Coosawhatchie. December 2, 1861.

> I received last night, dear Mary, your letter of the 12th, and am delighted to learn that you are all well and so many of you are together. I am much pleased that Fitzhugh has an opportunity to be with you all and will not be so far removed from his home in his new field of action. I hope to see him at the head of a find regiment and that he will be able to do good service in the cause of his country. If Mary and Rob get to you Christmas, you will have quite a family party, especially if Fitzhugh is not obliged to leave his home and sweet wife before that time. I shall think of you all on that holy day more intensely than usual, and shall pray to the great God of Heaven to shower His blessings upon

you in this world, and to unite you all in His courts in the world to come. With a grateful heart I thank Him for His preservation thus far, and trust to His mercy and kindness for the future. Oh, that I were more worthy, more thankful for all He has done and continues to do for me! Perry and Meredith [his two coloured servants] send their respects to all....

Truly and affectionately,

R. E. Lee.

Mary Anna Randolph Custis Lee was the great-granddaughter of Martha Custis Washington, step-great-granddaughter of George Washington, and daughter of George Washington Custis, the step-grandson and adopted son of George Washington. She was also the wife of Robert E. Lee

Engraving of Mary Anna Custis Lee, 1858
Library of Congress. Public Domain

To his daughter Annie:

From Coosawhatchie. December 8, 1861.

> *My Precious Annie: I have taken the only quiet time I have been able to find on this holy day to thank you for your letter of the 29th ulto. One of the miseries of war is that there is no Sabbath, and the current of work and strife has no cessation. How can we be pardoned for all our offenses! I am glad that you have joined your mamma again and that some of you are together at last. It would be a great happiness to me were you all at some quiet place, remote from the vicissitudes of war, where I could consider you safe. You must have had a pleasant time at 'Clydale.' I hope indeed that 'Cedar Grove' may be saved from the ruin and pillage that other places have received at the hands of our enemies, who are pursuing the same course here as they have practised elsewhere. Unfortunately, too, the numerous deep estuaries, all accessible to their ships, expose the multitude of islands to their predatory excursions, and what they leave is finished by the negroes whose masters have deserted their plantations, subject to visitations of the enemy. I am afraid Cousin Julia [Mrs. Richard Stuart] will not be able to defend her home if attacked by the vandals, for they have little respect for anybody, and if they catch the Doctor [Doctor Richard Stuart] they will certainly send him to Fort Warren or La Fayette. I fear, too, the Yankees will bear off their pretty daughters. I am very glad you visited 'Chatham' [the home of the Fitzhughs, where my grandmother Custis was born]. I was there many years ago, when it was the residence of Judge Coulter, and some of*

the avenues of poplar, so dear to your grandmama, still existed. I presume they have all gone now. The letter that you and Agnes wrote from 'Clydale' I replied to and sent to that place. You know I never have any news. I am trying to get a force to make headway on our defenses, but it comes in very slow. The people do not seem to realise that there is a war. It is very warm here, if that is news, and as an evidence I inclose some violets I plucked in the yard of a deserted house I occupy. I wish I could see you and give them in person.... Good-bye, my precious child. Give much love to everybody, and believe me,

Your affectionate father,

R. E. Lee.

Anne Carter Lee

Find A Grave Memorial
https://www.findagrave.com/memorial/8090573/anne-carter-lee

To his wife:

From Coosawhatchie. Christmas Day,1861.

> *I cannot let this day of grateful rejoicing pass, dear Mary, without some communication with you. I am thankful for the many among the past that I have passed with you, and the remembrance of them fills me with pleasure. For those on which we have been separated we must not repine. Now we must be content with the many blessings we receive. If we can only become sensible of our transgressions, so as to be fully penitent and forgiven, that this heavy punishment under which we labour may with justice be removed from us and the whole nation, what a gracious consummation of all that we have endured it will be!*
>
> *I hope you had a pleasant visit to Richmond.... If you were to see this place, I think you would have it, too. I am here but little myself. The days I am not here I visit some point exposed to the enemy, and after our dinner at early candle-light, am engaged in writing till eleven or twelve o'clock at night.... AS to our old home, if not destroyed, it will be difficult ever to be recognised. Even if the enemy had wished to preserve it, it would almost have been impossible. With the number of troops encamped around it, the change of officers, etc., the want of fuel, shelter, etc., and all the dire necessities of war, it is vain to think of its being in a habitable condition. I fear, too, books, furniture, and the relics of Mount Vernon will be gone. It is better to make up our minds to a general loss. They cannot take away the remembrance of the*

spot, and the memories of those that to us rendered it sacred. That will remain to us as long as life will last, and that we can preserve. In the absence of a home, I wish I could purchase 'Stratford.' That is the only other place that I could go to, now accessible to us, that would inspire me with feelings of pleasure and local love. You and the girls could remain there in quiet. It is a poor place, but we could make enough cornbread and bacon for our support, and the girls could weave us clothes. I wonder if it is for sale and at how much. Ask Fitzhugh to try to find out, when he gets to Fredericksburg. You must not build your hopes on peace on account of the United States going into a war with England [on account of the Trent affair]. She will be very loath to do that, notwithstanding the bluster of the Northern papers. Her rulers are not entirely mad, and if they find England is in earnest, and that war or a restitution of their captives must be the consequence, they will adopt the latter. We must make up our minds to fight our battles and win our independence alone. No one will help us. We require no extraneous aid, if true to ourselves. But we must be patient. It is not a light achievement and cannot be accomplished at once.... I wrote a few days since, giving you all the news, and have now therefore nothing to relate. The enemy is still quiet and increasing in strength. We grow in size slowly but are working hard. I have had a day of labour instead of rest, and have written intervals to some of the children. I hope they are with you, and inclose my letters....

Affectionately and truly,

R. E. Lee

To his wife:

From Coosawhatchie. January 18, 1862.

> *On my return, day before yesterday, from Florida, dear Mary, I received your letter of the 1st inst. I am very glad to find that you had a pleasant family meeting Christmas, and that it was so large. I am truly grateful for all the mercies we enjoy, notwithstanding the miseries of war, and join heartily in the wish that the next year may find us at peace with all the world. I am delighted to hear that our little grandson [his first grandchild—son of my brother Fitzhugh. He died in 1863] is improving so fast and is becoming such a perfect gentleman. May his path be strewn with flowers and his life with happiness. I am very glad to hear also that his dear papa is promoted. It will be gratifying to him and increase, I hope, his means of usefulness. Robert wrote me he saw him on his way through Charlottesville with his squadron, and that he was well. While at Fernandina I went over to Cumberland Island and walked up to 'Dungeness,' the former residence of General Green. It was my first visit to the house, and I had the gratification at length of visiting my father's grave. He died there, you may recollect, on his way from the West Indies, and was interred in one corner of the family cemetery. The spot is marked by a plain marble slab, with his name, age, and her daughter, Mrs. Shaw, and her husband. The place is at present owned by Mr. Nightingale, nephew of Mrs. Shaw, who married a daughter of Mr. James King. The family have moved into the*

interior of Georgia, leaving only a few servants and a white gardener on the place. The garden was beautiful, inclosed by the finest hedge I have ever seen. It was of the wild olive, which, in Mrs. Shaw's lifetime, during my tour of duty in Savannah in early life, was so productive, had been destroyed by an insect that has proved fatal to the orange on the coast of Georgia and Florida. There was a fine grove of olives, from which, I learn, Mr. Nightingale procures oil. The garden was filled with roses and beautiful vines, the names of which I do not know. Among them was the tomato-vine in full bearing, with the ripe fruit on it. There has yet been no frost in that region of country this winter. I went in the dining-room and parlour, in which the furniture still remained.... The house has never been finished, but is a fine, large one and beautifully located. A magnificent grove of live-oaks envelops the road from the landing to the house.... Love to everybody and God bless you all.

Truly and faithfully yours,

R. E. Lee.

To his wife:

From Coosawhatchie. January 28, 1862.

> I have just returned from Charleston, and received your letter of the 14th, dear Mary.... I was called to Charleston by the appearance off the bar of a fleet of vessels the true character and intent of which could not be discerned during the continuance of the storm which obscured the view. Saturday, however, all doubt was dispelled, and from the beach on Sullivan's Island the preparations for sinking them were plainly seen. Twenty-one were visible the first day of my arrival, but at the end of the storm, Saturday, only seventeen were seen. Five of these were vessels of war: what became of the other four is not known. The twelve old merchantmen were being stripped of their spars, masts, etc., and by sunset seven were prepared apparently for sinking across the mouth of the Maffitt Channel, they were placed in a line about two hundred yards apart, about four miles from Fort Moultrie. They will do but little harm to the channel, I think, but may deter vessels from running out at night for fear of getting on them. There now seem to be indications of a movement against Savannah. The enemy's gunboats are pushing up the creek to cut off communication between the city and Fort Pulaski on Cockspur Island. Unless I have better news, I must go there to-day. There are so many points of attack, and so little means to meet them on the water, that

> there is but little rest.... Perry and Meredith are well and send regards to everybody....
>
> Very truly and sincerely yours,
>
> R. E. Lee.

To his wife:

From Savannah. February 8, 1862.

> I wrote to you, dear Mary, the day I left Coosawhatchie for this place. I have been here ever since, endeavouring to push forward the work for the defense of the city, which has lagged terribly and which ought to have been finished. But it is difficult to arouse ourselves from ease and comfort to labour and self-denial. Guns are scarce, as well as ammunition, and I shall have to break up batteries on the coast to provide, I fear, for this city. Our enemies are endeavouring to work their way through the creeks that traverse the impassable marshes stretching along the interior of the coast and communicating with the sounds and sea, through which the Savannah flows, and thus avoid the entrance of the river commanded by Fort Pulaski. Their boats require only seven feet of water to float them, and the tide rises seven feet, so that at high water they can work their way and rest on the mud at low. They are also provided with dredges and appliances for removing obstructions through the creeks in question, which cannot be guarded by batteries. I hope, however, we shall be able to stop them, and I daily pray to the Giver of all victories to enable us to

> do so.... I trust you are all well and doing well, and wish I could do anything to promote either. I have more here than I can do, and more, I fear, than I can well accomplish. It is so very hard to get anything done, and while all wish well and mean well, it is so different to get them to act energetically and promptly.... The news from Kentucky and Tennessee is not favourable, but we must make up our minds to meet with reverses and overcome them. I hope God will at last crown our efforts with success. But the contest must be long and severe, and the whole country has to go through much suffering. It is necessary we should be humbled and taught to be less boastful, less selfish, and more devoted to right and justice to all the world....
>
> Always yours,
>
> R. E. Lee.

To his wife:

From Savannah. February 23, 1862.

> I have been wishing, dear Mary, to write to you for more than a week, but every day and every hour seem so taken up that I have found it impossible.... The news from Tennessee and North Carolina is not all cheering, and disasters seem to be thickening around us. It calls for renewed energies and redoubled strength on our part, and, I hope, will produce it. I fear our soldiers have not realised the necessity for the endurance and labour they are called upon to undergo, and that it is better to sacrifice themselves

than our cause. God, I hope, will shield us and give us success. Here the enemy is progressing slowly in his designs, and does not seem prepared, or to have determined when or where to make his attack. His gunboats are pushing up all the creeks and marshes of the Savannah, and have attained a position so near the river as to shell the steamers navigating it. None have as yet been struck. I am engaged in constructing a line of defense at Fort Jackson which, if time permits and guns can be obtained, I hope will keep them out. They can bring such overwhelming force in all their movements that it has the effect to demoralise our new troops. The accounts given in the papers of the quantity of cotton shipped to New York are, of course, exaggerated. It is cotton in the seed and dirt, and has to be ginned and cleaned after its arrival. It is said that the negroes are employed in picking and collecting it, and are paid a certain amount. But all these things are gathered from rumour, and can only be believed as they appear probable, which this seems to be.... I went yesterday to church, being the day appointed for fasting and prayer. I wish I could have passed it more devoutly. The bishop (Elliott) gave a most beautiful prayer for the President, which I hope may be heard and answered.... Here the yellow jasmine, red-bud, orange-tree, etc., perfume the whole woods, and the japonicas and azaleas cover the garden. Perry and Meredith are well.

May God bless and keep you always is the constant prayer of your husband,

R. E. Lee.

To his daughter Annie:

From Savannah. March 2, 1862.

> *My Precious Annie: It has been a long time since I have written to you, but you have been constantly in my thoughts. I think of you all, separately and collectively, in the busy hours of the day and the silent hours of the night, and the recollection of each one whiles away the long night, in which my anxious thoughts drive away sleep. But I always feel that you and Agnes at those times are sound asleep, and that is immaterial to either where the blockaders are or what their progress is in the river. I hope you are all well, and as happy as you can be in these perilous times to our country. They look dark at present, and it is plain we have not suffered enough, laboured enough, repented enough, to deserve success. But they will brighten after awhile, and I trust that a merciful God will arouse us to a sense of our danger, bless our honest efforts, and drive back our enemies to their homes. Our people have not been earnest enough, have thought too much of themselves and their ease, and instead of turning out to a man, have been content to nurse themselves and their dimes, and leave the protection of themselves and families to others. To satisfy their consciences, they have been clamorous in criticising what others have done, and endeavoured to prove that they ought to do nothing. This is not the way to accomplish our independence. I have been doing all I can with our small means and slow workmen to defend the cities and coast here.*

Against ordinary numbers we are pretty strong, but against the hosts our enemies seem able to bring everywhere there is no calculating. But if our men will stand to their work, we shall give them trouble and damage them yet. They have worked their way across the marshes, with their dredges, under cover of their gunboats, to the Savannah River, about Fort Pulaski. I presume they will endeavour to reduce the fort and thus open a way for their vessels up the river. But we have an interior line they must force before reaching the city. It is on this line we are working, slowly to my anxious mind, but as fast as I can drive them.... Good-bye, my dear child. May God bless you and our poor country.

Your devoted father,

R. E. Lee

After writing the above letter to Annie, Lee was recalled to Richmond, Virginia, "and was assigned on the 13th of March, under the direction of the President, to the conduct of the military operations of all the armies of the Confederate States".

Source: *Recollections and Letters of General Robert E. Lee. Chapter III-Letters to Wife and Daughters.* By Captain Robert E. Lee, Jr. [1]

Captain Robert E. Lee, Jr.

Courtesy of Arlington House, the Robert E. Lee Memorial

Chapter 20

First United States Colored Troops

The First South Carolina Volunteer Infantry was the first officially recognized black unit of the Union Army during the Civil War. It was quietly authorized by President Abraham Lincoln and organized in Beaufort, South Carolina, in August of 1862. The regiment reached its full complement of 1,000 men and was mustered in during November of that year. Most of the men were former slaves who had escaped from South Carolina and Florida. They came to Beaufort when the Federal army gained control of the city. The regiment's first commander was Thomas Wentworth Higginson. Like all the officers, he was white.

When informed of the regiment's organization, Confederate President Jefferson Davis ordered that any captured members were not to be considered prisoners of war. The enlisted men would be treated as slaves. They would be returned to their owners or auctioned off by state authorities. The white officers, however, were to be treated differently. They were to be hanged.

Following the war, Colonel Higginson wrote,

We, their officers, did not go there to teach lessons, but to receive them. There were more than a hundred men in the ranks who had voluntarily met more dangers in their escape from slavery than any of my young captains had incurred in all their lives." The regiment was particularly effective at conducting raids along the coast of Florida and Georgia, due to their familiarity with the terrain.

1st S.C. Colored Volunteer Infantry Regiment.

Taken from *War-Time Letters From Seth Rogers, M.D. Surgeon of the First South Carolina Afterwards the Thirty-third U.S.C.T,* Florida History Online, 1862-1863.

Wikipedia states,

The regiment was a step in the evolution of Union thinking towards the escaped slaves who crossed their lines. Initially they were returned to their owners. Next they were considered contraband and employed as laborers. Finally the legal fiction that they were property was abandoned and they were allowed to enlist in the Army, although in segregated units commanded by white officers. Harriet Tubman served with these men as a cook, nurse, spy, and scout. Susie King Taylor, whose husband and other relatives fought with the regiment, also served as a laundress and nurse for the men from August 1862 until mustering out on February 9, 1866. As a holdover from the "contraband" days, black privates were paid $10 per month, the rate for laborers, rather than the $13 paid to white privates. The men served as the precedent for the over 170,000 *"colored" troops* who followed them into the Union Army.

Col. Higginson, a minister, author and abolitionist, documented the Gullah dialect spoken by the men and made a record of the *spirituals* that they sang. Captain Seth Rogers was regimental surgeon and wrote extensive war time letters. His nephew, Captain James Seth Rogers, previously of the 51st Massachusetts, was captain of Company B.

The regiment was re-designated the 33rd United States Colored Infantry Regiment on February 8, 1864. [1]

The freed men and women shown outside their dwellings were formerly enslaved at the J.J. Smith Plantation on Port Royal Island, South Carolina. The Smith Plantation was confiscated by Federal forces and converted to a training camp for the United States Colored Infantry. Colonel Thomas Wentworth Higginson's regiment, the First South Carolina Volunteers, was encamped there in 1862 and 1863. Library of Congress.

Chapter 21

Federal Victory

The Federal troops attempted to destroy the Pocotaligo, Tulifinny, and Coosawhatchie railroad bridges on October 21-22, 1862. General Robert E. Lee was in command, and their attacks were a complete failure.

But three years later, during Sherman's "March to the Sea," the tide had turned. The following news articles reported the Federal victories, the Confederate victory at Honey Hill near Grahamville, and the exchange of prisoners.

The Pocotaligo, S.C. Railroad Bridge.

The Civil War In My South

Theodore R. Davis' drawing was published in *Harper's Weekly* on February 25, 1865, page 113.

Civil War Reports on Battles at Pocotaligo and Honey Hill (Grahamville) S.C. December 3-12, 1864

The New York Times [1]

> GEN. FOSTER'S OPERATIONS.; CAPTURE OF POCOTALIGO BRIDGE. The Savannah and Charleston Railroad Cut. SAVANNAH COMPLETELY ISOLATED. Foster's Scouts Said to be in Communication with Sherman. THE EXCHANGE OF PRISONERS.
>
> From Our Special Correspondent. Dec. 13, 1864
>
> PHILADELPHIA, Monday, Dec. 12.
>
> The Bulletin has the following important intelligence:
>
> The steamer Donegal arrived here this afternoon from the South Atlantic Blockading Squadron, having left Port Royal on the 7th inst.
>
> The joint naval and land expedition, under Admiral DAHLGREN and Gen. FOSTER, proceeded from Beaufort, up the Broad River, on Tuesday, Dec. 6, the object being to destroy the Pocotaligo Bridge, on the railroad between Charleston and Savannah.
>
> The Donegal accompanied the expedition to Telefaney Creek, but did not accompany it further.

There were seven gunboats in the expedition, and soon after reaching a proper position, a heavy fire was opened by them.

A force was landed, and action commenced.

Before evening, Pocotaligo Bridge was reached and destroyed.

Our troops were then intrenched for such future operations as might be needed.

The Donegal came down to Port Royal the same evening, but could not bring any details of the losses on either side.

Of the success of the grand object of the expedition, however, there can be no doubt.

Our informant speaks in the highest terms of the energy and activity of Admiral DAHLGREN in organizing and directing the movements of the naval brigade in this important affair.

When the Donegal left to come down Broad River on the evening of the 6th, shells were seen flying and exploding, which indicated that our forces were determined to drive the enemy out of any position they might have taken after being driven from the bridge.

Gen. FOSTER'S scouts had communicated with Gen. SHERMAN'S forces, which were marching on Savannah. The belief was that Gen. SHERMAN would be in Savannah on Wednesday, the 14th inst.

The Pocotaligo bridge is about thirty-five miles from Savannah. That bridge having been destroyed, and SHERMAN having cut the other railroad communications. Savannah cannot be relieved by reinforcements from any point north of the city.

From Our Special Correspondent.

OFF FORT SUMTER, CHARLESTON, S.C., Wednesday, Dec. 7, 1864.

The steamer Victor goes hence to-day with a few hundred released soldiers from the prison-pen at Florence, S.C. They were delivered to Col. MULFORD yesterday, and the aggregate number thus far received by us foot up 6,500. The remainder of the ten thousand are promised just as fast as they can be brought to Charleston, and Col. MULFORD hopes to close up the business here by the end of the present week, provided that the weather is favorable for the transhipment of the men in the open roadstead, near the ruins of Fort Sumter. Many of the released men are in the most deplorable condition, from sickness and privations.

Of SHERMAN's movement I can send you no news. The latest Charleston journals say that on Friday last he had passed through Millen, Ga., and there was no longer room to doubt that Savannah was his destination. I forward the latest flies of Charleston and Savannah journals. H.J.W.

Federal Victory

The flag-of-truce steamers from both sides met off Sullivan's Island at 12:30 P.M. The interview of the respective Commissioners lasted till 3 o'clock. We have not learned any particulars of the result, but believe that this harbor has been agreed upon as the point for the continuance of the exchange of prisoners recently begun in the Savannah River, but now, for obvious reasons, broken off at that point.

Lieut.-Col. W.H. HATCH and his Adjutant, Capt. M.J. O'BRIEN, of the Exchange Bureau, lately on a visit to Savannah, arrived in Charleston on Saturday afternoon. They were accompanied by Drs. BROCK and WILLIAMS, and the whole legation, with Mr. JOHN EDERS, Chairman of the Richmond Ambulance Committee. At 10 o'clock on Sunday morning, a flag-of-truce boat steamed down the harbor, in charge of Lieut-Col. HATCH, to the outer buoy, where he was met by Lieut.-Col. MULFORD. The interview of the Commissioners lasted till 3 o'clock.

The Courier says arrangements were made for a continued exchange of prisoners off this harbor. Col. MULFORD'S fleet, comprising some eight or ten vessels, are now lying outside of the harbor, preparatory to receiving prisoners. Another flag of truce will go down on Tuesday, with a number of Yankee prisoners. A number of officers, confined in Fort Pulaski, will probably be exchanged and returned to us at the same time. Under arrangements made with Col. MULFORD, there will be no shelling of the city during the stay of the Exchange Commissioner, which will probably be from two to three weeks. Col.

> HATCH has already turned over to Col. MULFORD, at Savannah, 5,500 prisoners, and will exchange about 5,000 more at this point.

FROM THE LINE OF THE SAVANNAH RAILROAD

> We have nothing additional of interest from the coast below. Passengers by the Savannah train which came in last evening reported that a fight was going on somewhere near Pocotaligo as they passed that point; but we were unable to gather any definite details in regard to the progress or result of the reported action. [1]

Chapter 22

Lee's Last Battle

Five days after Lee's men retreated from the trenches of Petersburg, Union Maj. Gen. Phil Sheridan's cavalry cut off three separate corps of Lee's army near Sailor's Creek. At the same time, the Union's Second and Sixth Corps advanced from the east.

On April 6th, two brigades of Andrew H. Humphrey's Second Corps overwhelmed two brigades of Maj. Gen. John B. Gordon's division as the Confederates struggled to move their supply and artillery trains across the creek.

Gordon's men were forced to make a stand at the Lockett family farm on the west bank. In a separate action, Lieut. Gen. Richard Anderson's Confederate infantry was attacked by Union cavalry under Maj. Gen. George Crook at Marshall's Crossroad, where the Yankee troopers blocked Anderson's route to join the other Confederate units.

The Union cavalry captured many of Anderson's artillery pieces near the creek, and most of Anderson's men fled the battlefield. In another fight, two divisions of Maj. Gen. Horatio Wright's Sixth

The Civil War In My South

Corps took up positions on the Hillsman farm north of Sailor's Creek opposite Gen. Richard S. Ewell's corps. Brig. Gen. Wesley Merritt's cavalry division engaged Ewell on Wright's left, cutting Ewell off from retreating west to Farmville and forcing the Confederate commander to surrender.

The Last Rally
Sayler's Creek, Virginia
April 6, 1865
Artwork by Mort Kunstler

Lee was at Rice's Station, where he listened to the sounds of artillery. He ordered General Mahone's Division to retrace their steps towards Sayler's Creek, and together, the two rode to a nearby hillside. One may only imagine Lee's thoughts as he gazed upon his panic-stricken soldiers.

Douglas Southall Freeman described the scene:

> *Lee spurred forward to rally the men who were running toward him. Either from the ground where the*

> bearer had dropped it in his flight, or else from the hand of some color-bearer, Lee took a battle flag and held it aloft. There on Traveller he sat, the red folds of the bunting flapping about him, the soldiers in a mob in front of him, some wild with fear, some exhausted, some wounded A few rushed on; others looked up and, recognizing him, began to flock around him as if to find shelter in his calm presence. Did it flash over him then that this was the last rally of the great Army of Northern Virginia? [1]

Lee knew that the end was not far off, not just for his army but also for the Confederacy. The Federals had captured 7,700 of Lee's men, resulting in roughly one-fourth of his army. Six Confederate generals, including Ewell, Joseph Kershaw, and Custis Lee, the commanding general's son, were captured.

Tamela Baker is a former editor of *America's Civil War*. In the March 2015 issue, she provided an excellent review of General Lee's efforts to avoid surrender. I have chosen to include it here in its entirety.

> ALL AROUND HIM, his soldiers were ragged and hungry. Desperate attempts in the last week to feed, clothe and arm them had been thwarted at every turn. Half his troops had been captured, killed or wounded—or had just left. Enemy armies surrounded him now; decision time had come.
>
> Robert E. Lee huddled with his commanders by a low bivouac in the south central Virginia countryside, the rooftops of the village of Appomattox Court House just visible above the tree line. "There

was no tent there, no table, no chairs, and no camp-stools," Maj. Gen. John Brown Gordon recalled. *"On blankets spread upon the ground or on saddles at the roots of the trees we sat around the great commander….No tongue or pen will ever be able to describe the unutterable anguish of Lee's commanders as they looked into the clouded face of their beloved leader and sought to draw from it some ray of hope."*

In the week since the fall of Petersburg and Richmond on April 3, Lee had been frantic to resupply his famished troops. Ultimately he hoped to combine the Army of Northern Virginia with Gen. Joseph Johnston's Army of Tennessee, now being tormented by William T. Sherman's Union forces in North Carolina. Lee went first to Amelia Court House, a stop on the Richmond & Danville Railroad, where he expected supplies from Richmond. But when food rations didn't appear, he headed for Jetersville to collect 200,000 rations sent from Danville. Federal troops got there first, however, so Lee opted for Farmville on the South Side Railroad. Intermittent fighting, fatigue and hunger, and the collapse of starving animals depleted his fighting force, which had numbered nearly 60,000 as they left Richmond and Petersburg.

The Battle of Sailor's Creek on April 6 took a particular toll, costing more than 8,000 troops in three engagements. Most were now prisoners of the Federals. Among them were a half-dozen general officers, including Richard Ewell and Lee's oldest son, Custis. "My God!" the elder Lee exclaimed as he saw survivors straggling from the fight, "has the army been dissolved?"

That was two days ago. Tonight, he didn't know what had become of Custis—or his youngest son, Rob, who had been captured as well. And yesterday, General Grant had invited Lee to surrender and avoid "further effusion of blood." Though he was unwilling to concede to Grant's opinion of the "hopelessness" of his cause, he wanted to keep his limited options open. He asked Grant for terms—not for surrender, but for peace—yet continued his retreat toward Danville. Supplies from Lynchburg were headed for Appomattox Station; once his men had some food, there might still be a chance to reach Johnston. Reserve artillery commanded by Brig. Gen. Reuben Lindsay Walker, halted near Appomattox Station to draw rations, was moving to Lynchburg; Walker's 100 guns were an impediment to a fleeing army.

But the Federals heard about Lee's supply trains, and Maj. Gen. George Custer descended with his cavalry on Appomattox Station—where he found four trains and Walker's artillery. Surprised and disorganized, the Confederates were stubborn nonetheless. By nightfall, however, the Federals had captured 1,000 more of Lee's dwindling forces, three of the supply trains, 25 guns, scores of wagons and up to 300,000 (accounts vary) of the Rebels' precious food rations. Most of Walker's artillery escaped to the north and west, but were scattered and therefore useless.

To Lee's further consternation, Federal cavalry rushed onto the Lynchburg–Richmond Stage Road and charged into nearby Appomattox Court House, cutting off Lee's escape route. Everywhere he looked, there were Federals. Today he had asked Grant for a conversation.

I cannot...meet you with a view to surrender the Army of Northern Virginia, but as far as your proposal may affect the C.S. forces under my command, and tend to the restoration of peace, I should be pleased to meet you at 10 a.m., to-morrow; on the old stage road to Richmond, between the picket-lines of the two armies.

He still hoped he could persuade Grant to discuss peace rather than surrender, but so far had no reply—or much encouragement Grant would see things his way.

Now, from his makeshift headquarters just northeast of the village, Lee knew he had only two choices: attack the Federals at dawn and try to break out, or surrender. He and his commanders—including Gordon, James Longstreet and Lee's nephew Fitzhugh—rested by the fire and considered each.

Maybe only Union cavalry stood between his army and escape. If he could break out, could the Confederate armies keep fighting until war-weary

Northerners let the Southern states go? If he surrendered, what would the fate of Southern people be?

"If all that was said and felt at that meeting could be given it would make a volume of measureless pathos," Gordon wrote. "In no hour of the great war did General Lee's masterful characteristics appear to me so conspicuous as they did in that last council. We knew by our own aching hearts that his was breaking. Yet he commanded himself, and stood calmly facing and discussing the long-dreaded inevitable."

After discussing both distasteful options, they decided to attack at daybreak. If it didn't work, then...

Many visitors don't realize there was fighting at Appomattox, says Patrick Schroeder, historian for Appomattox Court House National Historical Park. On a sunny autumn afternoon, Schroeder and other members of the park's staff are deep in preparations for the thousands of visitors anticipated during the sesquicentennial this spring. Five days of events are planned, including talks, tours, living history demonstrations and other activities. But Schroeder takes time out to tell a visitor about the nine days of events that brought the armies here.

"This campaign really is amazing because these troops are marching and fighting on a daily basis. It's unlike any other campaign, really," he observes. "This campaign doesn't have a Gettysburg, it doesn't have an Antietam, but there are smaller battles every day: Sutherland Station. Namozine

Church. Amelia Court House. Sailor's Creek. High Bridge. Cumberland Church. Here at Appomattox Station and then at Appomattox Court House. And in the course of the week Lee's army, which started out with about 60,000 men, has 30,000 men when it reaches Appomattox. Lee has lost half of his army in that weeklong march...and that is unparalleled in Civil War history."

That's roughly 10,000 killed or wounded, 10,000 captured—mainly at Sailor's Creek—and 10,000 deserters.

The Union army had been busy too, marching up to 30–35 miles per day—10 miles more than Stonewall Jackson's famed marchers—to cut Lee's army off before it could escape. By nightfall on April 8, Federal cavalry dug in less than a mile from the courthouse. Two cannon lobbed shells into the Confederate camp. Gordon's troops were just west of the village, preparing for the morning's do-or-die advance.

Early the next morning, Gordon's troops moved forward in wheel formation and scored initial success—capturing the two guns that had plagued the Rebels the night before, as well as some Yankee artillerymen. They hadn't counted on the appearance of infantry from the Union Army of the James, however, and as Gordon's forces were outmanned, the tide began to turn. As more and more Federal troops concentrated at Appomattox, Gordon sent a desperate message to his commander. "Tell General Lee that my command has been fought to a frazzle," he said, "and unless Longstreet can unite in the movement, or prevent these forces from coming upon my rear, I can not long go forward."

Longstreet, however, "was assailed by other portions of the Federal army," Gordon recalled. "He was so hardly pressed that he could not join, as contemplated, in the effort to break the cordon of men and metal around us."

Lee, according to his aide-de-camp Charles Venable, knew he was finished. "There is nothing left me but to go and see General Grant," he conceded, "and I had rather die a thousand deaths."

In the meantime, he had finally heard from Grant:

I have no authority to treat on the subject of peace; the meeting proposed for 10 a.m. to-day could lead to no good. I will state, however, general, that I am equally anxious for peace with yourself, and the whole North entertains the same feeling. The terms upon which peace can be had are well understood. By the South laying down their arms they will hasten that most desirable event, save thousands of human lives, and hundreds of millions of property not yet destroyed. Seriously hoping that all our difficulties may be settled without the loss of another life, I subscribe myself, &c.,

U.S. GRANT,

Lieutenant-General.

He sent for Longstreet, who found his commander dressed "in a suit of new uniform, sword and sash, a handsomely embroidered belt, boots, and a pair of gold spurs. He stood near the embers of some burned rails, received me with graceful salutation, and spoke at once of affairs in front and the loss of his subsistence stores...and, closing with the expression that it was not possible for him to get along, requested my view," Longstreet recalled. "I asked if the bloody sacrifice of his army could in any way help the cause in other quarters. He thought not. Then, I said, your situation speaks for itself.

Lee resigned himself to the task at hand.

Lieut. Gen. U.S. GRANT:

I received your note of this morning on the picket-line, whither I had come to meet you and ascertain definitely what terms were embraced in your proposal of yesterday with reference to the surrender of this army. I now ask an interview in accordance with the offer contained in your letter of yesterday for that purpose.

R.E. LEE,

General.

Grant, who had been nursing a headache since the day before, was riding a 22-mile circuit around the armies that morning. "I proceeded at an early hour in the morning, still suffering with the headache, to get to the head of the column. I was not more than two or three miles from Appomattox Court

House at the time, but to go direct I would have to pass through Lee's army, or a portion of it. I had therefore to move south in order to get upon a road coming up from another direction.

"When the officer reached me I was still suffering with the sick headache, but the instant I saw the contents of the note I was cured. I wrote the following note in reply and hastened on:

Your note of this date is but this moment (11.50 A.M.) received, in consequence of my having passed from the Richmond and Lynchburg road to the Farmville and Lynchburg road. I am at this writing about four miles west of Walker's Church and will push forward to the front for the purpose of meeting you.

After delivering Grant's message, Union Lt. Col. Orville E. Babcock escorted Lee and his aide, Lt. Col. Charles Marshall, into the village of Appomattox Court House. Marshall, sent ahead to find a suitable place for the meeting, soon happened on Wilmer McLean—a sugar speculator who had left his home in Manassas after the two battles there and was living in the village. McLean first showed him to an empty building, but when Marshall passed on that venue, McLean offered his home.

Lee arrived at the McLean House at about 1 p.m. to surrender the depleted remainder of his army— an army once proud and defiant, and not without reason. They had scared George McClellan off the Virginia Peninsula, humiliated Ambrose Burnside at Fredericksburg and flustered Joe Hooker at Chancellorsville. Nobody could say they hadn't taken their best shot. But now, so many were gone. Stonewall. Jeb. And just last week, A.P. Hill.

Lee stepped into Wilmer McLean's parlor and waited.

Although many original Appomattox Court House structures remain, some have been lost and some—the courthouse and the McLean House itself—have been restored. The courthouse burned in 1892, destroying records and prompting residents to build a new structure at Appomattox Station, now known simply as Appomattox. But during the Civil War centennial, the former courthouse was rebuilt and now serves as the visitor center for the national park. The McLean House, vacated by the McLeans in 1867, was sold in 1891 to a Niagara Falls, N.Y., development firm to be dismantled and moved to Washington for permanent display. But a financial panic—and the company's resulting bankruptcy—quashed those plans, and the building materials remained on the property until the park service rebuilt the house in the late 1940s. When it was dedicated in 1950, Ulysses Grant III and Robert E. Lee IV attended.

Grant and Lee found a village boasting activity that can only be imagined now. The Clover Hill Tavern had a dining wing that has since disappeared. There were two general stores, only one of which remains, and some offices (two are left), and the northeast side of the Richmond-Lynchburg Stage

Road was lined with the shops of the Rosser family enterprises.

"Lee comes up here, he gets here about 1 o'clock… Grant arrives about a half-hour later," Schroeder explains. "People like to make a big deal about 'Grant was all mud-splattered' and stuff like that. Well, the thing is, you've got to understand the situation. Lee had put on a new uniform and rode a little over a mile from his headquarters. Grant rode 22 miles over Virginia roads in April, after it's been raining a lot. Not only was Grant mud-splattered, his whole staff was mud-splattered.

"Grant was never a fancy dresser to begin with, but that was the situation at hand. He told Lee that he didn't have time to go to his baggage wagon… but Lee said that he was glad he came when he did. Because [Lee] had to sit there and think over things by himself. Many people write about what he was thinking…but we don't know what Lee was thinking about."

The meeting between Grant and Lee ended at about 3 p.m.—the time frozen on the clock at the McLean House, one of the few pieces of family furnishings still there. (Tamela Baker)

There was, of course, much to contemplate. Lee had met Grant before, during the Mexican War. But in this war, Grant had established a fearsome reputation as "Unconditional Surrender" Grant. Or, among those repulsed by the body count in his wake, "Grant the Butcher." And he was the only

Union general who pursued Lee with such tenacity. Lee could be forgiven for whatever anxiety he felt.

Grant arrived at around 1:30 p.m. "We greeted each other, and after shaking hands took our seats," Grant recalled. "What General Lee's feelings were I do not know. As he was a man of much dignity, with an impassible face, it was impossible to say whether he felt inwardly glad that the end had finally come, or felt sad over the result, and was too manly to show it. Whatever his feelings, they were entirely concealed from my observation; but my own feelings, which had been quite jubilant on the receipt of his letter, were sad and depressed. I felt like anything rather than rejoicing at the downfall of a foe who had fought so long and valiantly, and had suffered so much for a cause, though that cause was, I believe, one of the worst for which a people ever fought.

"...We soon fell into a conversation about old army times. He remarked that he remembered me very well in the old army; and I told him that as a matter of course I remembered him perfectly, but from the difference in our rank and years (there being about sixteen years' difference in our ages), I had thought it very likely that I had not attracted his attention sufficiently to be remembered by him after such a long interval. Our conversation grew so pleasant that I almost forgot the object of our meeting. After the conversation had run on in this style for some time, General Lee called my attention to the object of our meeting.

Lee asked Grant to put his terms in writing; Grant asked for writing materials, then composed a concise proviso.

GEN: In accordance with the substance of my letter to you of the 8th inst., I propose to receive the surrender of the Army of N. Va. on the following terms, to wit: Rolls of all the officers and men to be made in duplicate. One copy to be given to an officer designated by me, the other to be retained by such officer or officers as you may designate. The officers to give their individual paroles not to take up arms against the Government of the United States until properly exchanged, and each company or regimental commander sign a like parole for the men of their commands. The arms, artillery and public property to be parked and stacked, and turned over to the officer appointed by me to receive them. This will not embrace the side-arms of the officers, nor their private horses or baggage. This done, each officer and man will be allowed to return to their homes, not to be disturbed by United States authority so long as they observe their paroles and the laws in force where they may reside.

Very respectfully,

U.S. GRANT,
Lt. Gen.

"When I put my pen to the paper I did not know the first word that I should make use of in writing the terms," Grant wrote in his memoirs. "I only knew *what was in my mind, and I wished to express it clearly, so that there could be no mistaking it. As I wrote on, the thought occurred to me that the officers had their own private horses and effects, which were important to them, but of no value to us; also that it would be an unnecessary humiliation to call upon them to deliver their side arms.... When he read over that part of the terms about side arms, horses and private property of the officers, he remarked, with some feeling, I thought, that this would have a happy effect upon his army."*

After some brief clarifications, it was Lee's turn to compose a response.

GENERAL:—I received your letter of this date containing the terms of the surrender of the Army of Northern Virginia as proposed by you. As they are substantially the same as those expressed in your letter of the 8th inst., they are accepted. I will proceed to designate the proper officers to carry the stipulations into effect.

R.E. LEE, General.

Lee had one more bit of business to transact: His men were hungry. Phil Sheridan's cavalry, after all, had captured his rations. Grant told him to send his quartermaster to get all the provisions needed. "After that a general conversation took place of a most agreeable character," Marshall recalled. "I cannot describe it. I cannot give you any idea of the kindness, and generosity, and magnanimity of those men. When I think of it, it brings tears into my eyes.

"After having this general conversation we took leave of General Grant, and went off to appoint commissioners to attend to the details of the surrender."

"As General Lee rode back to his army the officers and soldiers of his troops about the front lines assembled in promiscuous crowds of all arms and grades in anxious wait for their loved commander," Longstreet wrote in his memoirs. *"From force of habit a burst of salutations greeted him, but quieted as suddenly as they arose. The road was packed with standing troops as he approached, the men with hats off, heads and hearts bowed with standing men. As he passed they raised their heads and looked upon him with swimming eyes. Those who could find voice said good-by, those who could not speak, and were near, passed their hands gently over the sides of Traveller. He rode with his hat off, and had sufficient control to fix his eyes on a line between the ears of Traveller and look neither to right nor left until he reached a large white-oak tree, where he dismounted to make his last Headquarters, and finally talked a little."*

After tending to some clerical details, Grant sent a telegram to Secretary of War Edwin Stanton:

General Lee surrendered the Army of Northern Virginia this afternoon on terms proposed by myself.

The accompanying additional correspondence will show the conditions fully.

U. S. GRANT,

Lieut.-General.

Grant and Lee met again the following day. Grant attempted to persuade Lee to surrender all Confederate armies. "But Lee said that he could not do that without consulting the President first," Grant remembered. "I knew there was no use to urge him to do anything against his ideas of what was right."

Neither commander participated in the formal surrender, leaving their subordinates to carry out the details. Grant sped to Washington, with his assistant adjutant Captain Robert Todd Lincoln—the president's eldest son—close behind, "with a view to putting a stop to the purchase of supplies, and what I now deemed other useless outlay of money."

He would also meet with the president, and get an invitation to the theater. Chilly relations between Julia Grant and the First Lady would prompt the Grants to decline.

Lee remained in the vicinity of Appomattox for a few more days. Eventually, he broke camp and climbed onto Traveller for the long ride back to Richmond. [2]

General Johnston surrendered to General Sherman at Bentonville upon receiving word of General Lee's surrender. The war was over.

Chapter 23

Final Engagements of the S.C. Confederate Lowcountry Troops

January 1865

3. Skirmish near Hardeeville.

14. Advance of Union forces from Beaufort to Pocotaligo and skirmishes.

15. Destruction of the U.S. monitor Patapsco, in Charleston Harbor.

20. Reconnaissance from Pocotaligo to the Salkehatchie River, and skirmish.

25. Reconnaissance from Pocotaligo to the Salkehatchie River.

26. Skirmish at Pocotaligo.

27. Skirmish at Ennis' Cross Roads.

28. Skirmish at Combahee River.

The Civil War In My South

29. Skirmish at Robertville.

30. Skirmish near Lawtonville. (now Estill, S.C.)

February 1865

1. Skirmish at Hickory Hill and Skirmish at Whippy Swamp.

2. Skirmish at Lawtonville.
   Skirmish at Barker's Mill, Whippy Swamp.
   Skirmish at Duck Branch, near Loper's Cross Roads.
   Skirmishes at Rivers' and Broxton's Bridges, Salkehatchie River.

3. Action at Rivers' Bridge, Salkehatchie River.
   Skirmish at Dillingham's Cross Roads or Duck Branch.

4. Skirmish at Angley's Post Office.
   Skirmish at Buford's Bridge.

5. Skirmish at Duncanville.
   Skirmish at Combahee Ferry.

6. Action at Fishburn's Plantation, near Lane's Bridge, Little Salkehatchie River.
   Skirmish at Cowpen Ford, Little Salkehatchie River.
   Skirmish near Barnwell.

7. Skirmish at Blackville.
   Skirmish at the Edisto Railroad Bridge.
   Reconnaissance to Cannon's Bridge, South Edisto River.

8. Skirmish at Williston.
   Skirmish near White Pond.

Skirmish at Walker's or Valley Bridge, Edisto River.
Skirmish at Cannon's Bridge, South Edisto River.

9. Skirmish at Binnaker's Bridge, South Edisto River.
Skirmish at Holman's Bridge, South Edisto River.

10. Skirmish at James Island.
Skirmish at Johnson's Station.

11. Action at Aiken.
Action at Johnson's Station.
Attack on Battery Simkins.
Action neat Sugar Loaf, NC.

11-12th. Skirmishes about Orangeburg.
12-13th. Skirmishes at the North Edisto River.

14. Skirmish at Wolf's Plantation.
Skirmish at Gunter's Bridge, North Edisto River.

15. Skirmish at Congaree Creek.
Skirmish at Savannah Creek.
Skirmish at Bate's Ferry, Congaree River.
Skirmish at Red Bank Creek.
Skirmish at Two League Cross Roads, near Lexington.

16-17th. Skirmishes about Columbia.

17th. Union Forces occupy Columbia.

March 1865

7-10. Wyse Fork.

10. Monroe's Cross Roads.

16. Averasborough

19. Bentonville.

April 1865

General Joseph E. Johnston met with President Jefferson Davis in Greensboro, North Carolina, in April 1865. During that meeting, he told the Confederate president,

> *Our people are tired of the war, feel themselves whipped, and will not fight. Our country is overrun, its military resources greatly diminished, while the enemy's military power and resources were never greater and may be increased to any extent desired. ,,, My small force is melting away like snow before the sun.*

On April 26, Johnston, knowing that Lee had surrendered, formally surrendered to Sherman his army and Confederate forces in North Carolina, South Carolina, Georgia, and Florida.

Source: *Historical Sketch And Roster Of The South Carolina 3rd Cavalry Regiment* by John C. Rigdon. Pages 55-61. [1]

Chapter 24

The Civil War and Christianity

Most historians have ignored the importance of Christianity during the Civil War. One exception is Gardiner H. Shattuck, Jr. He wrote,

> *The single aspect of the war that the National Park Service has failed to highlight is the impact of religion on the soldiers. Orientation films and shows at visitor centers never note how important religion was...Civil War soldiers gathered in great numbers around campfires to participate in revivals, not just to see minstrel shows.* [1]

Massive revivals occurred among the Federal and Confederate soldiers. There were hundreds of thousands of conversions. Chapels were packed night after night. How could they not be? When one faces his death at any moment, one considers his relationship with his Creator with urgency.

During the Civil War, the three largest Christian denominations were the Presbyterians, Methodists, and Baptists. All of them split over slavery and related issues. South Carolina's Senator John C. Calhoun knew that these denominations "formed a strong cord to hold the Union together." When the split did take place, he prophesied that "nothing will be left to hold the States together except force."

There were three to four million slaves in America. Most, but not all, were in the Confederate states. How did they endure their years of forced servitude? Most of them were Christians. I suppose the Holy Bible's Book of Exodus held great significance for them. They continued to trust that Jesus Christ would sustain them and rescue them from their bondage one day.

Among the leaders of the Confederate and Federal armies were Christian Generals. For the Confederates, the most well-known were: Robert E. Lee, "Stonewall" Jackson, William Pendleton, and Leonides Polk. Federal leadership included Generals Oliver O. Howard, George B. McClellan, William Rosecrans, and Ulysses S. Grant.

Renowned Christian ministers in the North and South found scriptural grounds to support their causes. Their ardent preaching that the Bible justified the war gained popular support on both sides. That support continued until the war ended with six hundred thousand lives lost. (A more accurate estimate of Civil War deaths is about 750,000, ranging from 650.000 to as many as 850,000 dead). [2]

Little-known Facts About Christianity During the Civil War

1. Major revivals broke out in the Civil War armies. In the Union Army, between 100,000 and 200,000 soldiers were converted; among Confederate forces, approximately 150,000 troops

The Civil War and Christianity

converted to Christ. Perhaps 10 percent of all Civil War soldiers experienced conversions during the conflict.

2. Though he knew the Bible thoroughly and spoke often of an Almighty God, Abraham Lincoln was never baptized and was the only United States president never to join a church.

3. By 1860, there were nearly 4,000,000 slaves in the United States. One of every seven Americans belonged to another. (Yet most Confederate soldiers didn't own any slaves.)

4. Before 1830, many leaders in the anti-slavery movement came from the South.

5. Three of the nation's leading Protestant denominations- the Presbyterians, Methodists, and Baptists- divided over slavery and other related issues. These church divisions fractured political parties and ultimately helped to divide the nation.

6. As early as 1818, Presbyterians unanimously declared at their General Assembly that "the voluntary enslaving of one part of the human race by another" is "utterly inconsistent with the law of God." Ironically, however, the same assembly upheld the decision to depose a Presbyterian minister because he held anti-slavery views. And in 1845, the General Assembly agreed that slavery was a biblical institution.

7. A "Great Revival" occurred among Robert E. Lee's forces in the fall of 1863 and winter of 1864. Some 7,000 soldiers were converted. Revivals also swept the Union Army at that time. Sometimes preaching and praying continued 24 hours a day, and chapels couldn't hold the soldiers who wanted to get inside.

The Civil War In My South

8. Chapels often were built in soldiers' quarters. In 1864, the Army of Northern Virginia alone boasted 15 chapels. One chapel built by the Army of Tennessee seated more than 1,000 people.

9. Before the Civil War, it was rare to find chaplains in American armies. During the war, they earned a lasting place.

10. The Constitution of the Confederate States of America specifically invoked "Almighty God"-unlike the Constitution of the Union. Further, the Confederate Constitution prohibited the foreign slave trade.

11. Millions of tracts were distributed to soldiers during the war. (Average price: 1,500 for $1.) The U.S. Christian Commission alone distributed 30 million tracts, including many through a young agent named Dwight L. Moody.

12. Christians who opposed the war on religious grounds were often persecuted. The Brethren eventually were exempted from military service if they paid $500, but most suffered for their stance. For example, John Kline, moderator of the Brethren Annual Meeting, became distrusted because he provided medical aid to soldiers from both armies. Once he was jailed for two weeks, without cause, and in June 1864, he was ambushed and murdered.

13. Blacks were not allowed to serve as chaplains (or soldiers) until 1863. Altogether, 14 black chaplains served U.S. regiments. One of the best known was H. M. Turner, whose preaching had drawn Congressmen to hear him; he was known as the "the Negro Spurgeon."

Source: *Christian History* Magazine. [3]

Chapter 25

Murder Most Foul

With the war finally over, my Great Grandfather George returned to Bluffton, where he continued a life of farming with his family. He and Eleanor had five additional children:

George, Liddia, Howard, Mitchell, and his twin, my Grandfather, Milledge. By all accounts, George and Eleanor were a nice couple. It seems they were respected by all who knew them.

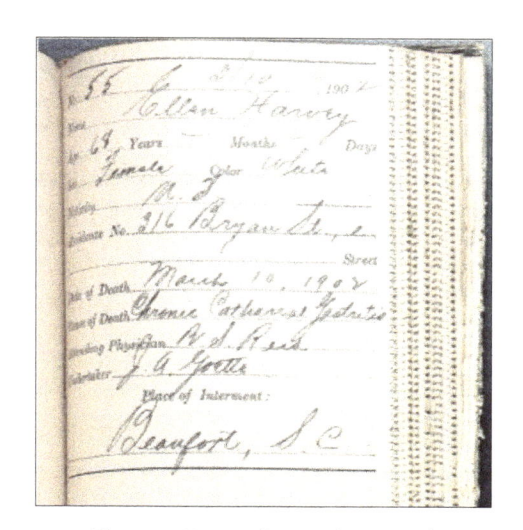

Eleanor Harvey's Death Record

Around 1901, Eleanor became ill. She was taken to Savannah, Georgia, to live with and be cared for by one of her daughters. She never recovered and died from Chronic Cathartic Gastritis on March 10, 1902. Her attending physician was R.S. Reid, M.D. The undertaker was J.A. Goette.

The State Newspaper published her short obituary on March 21, 1902,

> *Mrs. Eleanor Harvey, of Levy's, the esteemed wife of Mr. George M. Harvey, died in Savannah on the 10th instant. She had been ill for some time. The funeral took place at St. Luke's Church, at home, on the 11th. Her grave was covered with roses.* [1]

George had lost the love of his life. He continued to work on his farm and live one day at a time. By all accounts, George was a likable and respected gentleman. This was confirmed during the tragic last day of his life.

On August 16, 1906, he took a steamer from Bluffton to Ladies Island to visit his son Howard and his family. They resided at Sander's Plantation, where Howard was the manager.

Howard, with his family, had left the house to see some neighbors. When they returned home, they found George had been murdered. It was a Sunday afternoon, and George decided to nap on the veranda. He was 72.

With the help of Howard's black neighbors, it was soon determined that William Bennett was the perpetrator. Howard had hired Bennett as a plowman but had fired him due to his poor work and drinking. His termination occurred five days before he killed George.

The following newspaper articles provided the details of George's murder.

An Aged Citizen Brutally Killed

> Mr. George M. Harvey of Bluffton Foully Murdered.
>
> SHOT IN HIS SON'S HOME
>
> A Negro Arrested and Lodged in Beaufort Jail on Suspicion. No Fear of Lynching.
>
> Special to The State.
>
> Beaufort, Aug. 27. Mr. George M. Harvey was murdered Sunday night on Ladies Island. A negro is in the county jail, charged with the crime.
>
> The verdict of the coroner's jury was that deceased came to his death by a gun shot wound, the gun in the opinion of the jury being fired by Wm. Bennett, and that Wm. Ferguson is a material witness, if not accessory.
>
> Mr. Harvey, a well known farmer, age 72, of the Bluffton section, was visiting his son on a plantation on Ladies Island, four miles from Beaufort. Last evening he was left alone in the house from 5 until 7, and upon returning his son found him lying dead on the piazza with a horrible gunshot wound in

his head. A shotgun and pistol were missing from the house.

The gun has not been found, but this morning the sheriff found the pistol in a negro cabin where it had positively identified as having been left by Wm. Bennett, who was found on a public road soon after. He would admit nothing, but other neighbors testified they had seen him near the Harvey farm at the time the crime was committed and that he was drunk and in an ugly humor. The negro came from the up-country and was employed by Mr. Harvey as a plow hand up to Wednesday. The neighbors of the vicinity assisted in his capture and are much wrought up by what seems to be a brutal, unprovoked murder. The sheriff and a posse of citizens went to the scene early this morning. Though there was much feeling exhibited by the citizens present at the inquest, there was no danger of lynching. [2]

Murder Most Foul

The previous Sunday, August 26, George M. Harvey, a friendly Bluffton gentleman of 75 years, had traveled out to Lady's Island to visit with his son Howard H. Harvey and his family for the day. The younger Harvey managed the planting interests on W.F. Sander's farm. During the afternoon the younger Harvey family went out to visit neighbors, leaving Grandpa resting at the house. When they returned, they found Mr. George's brains had been shot out. A gun, originally reported as a pistol, and a shotgun belonging to Harvey were missing. Shortly thereafter the telephone rang at (Beaufort

County) Sheriff James McTeer's home on Charles Street. McTeer grabbed his trusted deputy Matty White, along with a posse of tried and true men, and headed up the river on a steamer to northern Lady's Island. The investigation didn't take long. The black citizens of Ladies Island were very disturbed by what they considered to be a brutal and unprovoked murder of a man they held in high regard. [3]

Negroes Gave Aid In Finding Criminal Circumstances Surrounding Killing of G.M. Harvey Somewhat Relieved by Attitude of Negroes

There are very few white families on this island and several thousand negroes. As soon as news of the tragedy spread Negroes on the plantation and from nearby settlements assisted young Mr. Harvey in caring for the dead and in securing information as to the possible perpetrator of the deed, which they all thought was William Bennett. Sam'l Green, a prosperous colored man of considerable influence among his people was particularly active and gave material assistance to the sheriff and the coroner. The Negroes expressed much indignation and made the capture of the prisoner now held possible.

These acts alleviated the possibility of violence leading to unlawful acts of retribution by white citizens. Their assistance to Sheriff McTeer directly led to the identification and capture of Bennett. He was taken into custody and brought to the jail on King Street, along with a material witness by the name of William Ferguson. Mr. Harvey was buried at St. Luke's Church on Bull Hill. [4]

Not long after Bennett was confined in the jail, Sheriff McTeer was informed a lynch mob was on the way from Ridgeland. One of George's sons, my grandfather Milledge Harvey, and my Great Uncle Rollin Cooler, worked at the jail as security officers. Along with my grandfather's brothers, they stood on the front steps of the jail and refused to let the mob take Bennett.

Chapter 26

Trial and Execution

On Monday, September 17, 1906, when Judge R.O. Purdy convened General Session Court in Beaufort, Solicitor Jervey presented indictments to the grand jury in six murder cases, including the case of William Bennett. The Grand Jury returned a true bill before lunch, and a trial was scheduled for Thursday. On the appointed day, the jury took their seats and heard a convincing argument from Solicitor Jervey. Before the sunset that evening, Bennett was found guilty of murder.

Beaufort County Courthouse. Circa 1920. Historic Resouces of the Lowcountry. Lowcountry Council of Governments. Yemassee, South Carolina. 1979.

The following day his attorneys petitioned the court for a new trial. Judge Purdy mulled the issue for a day and decided Bennett did deserve a new trial. He set a date for the following Tuesday.

According to the *Beaufort Gazette*, "The evidence was even more conclusive and convincing than the previous trial and the jury rendered a verdict of guilty." With the successful conclusion of the second trial, Judge Purdy passed sentence,

> *He should be taken to the place where he last came from, there be safely and securely held by the Sheriff until Friday, November 2, 1906 between the hours of 10 a.m. and 2 pm, where he should be taken to the place provided for execution and there be hanged by the neck until he was dead, and God have mercy on your soul.* [1]

On November 1, Sheriff McTeer announced that the scaffold was ready and that the execution would be carried out as ordered the following day. He did say that he would allow about twenty witnesses inside the jail yard to observe the event. It was the first execution by hanging in over six years in Beaufort County.

Sheriff McTeer gave the rope and noose used to hang Bennett to my Grandfather, Milledge Harvey. Milledge and his brother-in-law, Rollin Cooler, were employed by the Sheriff as jail guards. The rope was used at Harvey-Cooler family gatherings on the Okatie River as a source of remembrance and reflection for many years through the 1940s. Today, such behavior is considered inappropriate and unprofessional. But, this occurred in the early 1900s, only 40 years after the Civil War. It was a different era.

Trial and Execution

The governor later appointed Rollin Cooler as one of South Carolina's first State Constables. Sadly, he was also murdered in the line of duty on St. Helena Island on March 30, 1913.

United in life, George was now reunited with Eleanor in death. He was buried beside her at St. Luke's Cemetery on Bull Hill. The cemetery was known as "The Old Burying Ground."

The original site of St. Luke's Church at Bull Hill included the Church building and the cemetery where my Great Grandparents are buried. This church traced its roots to the mid-1700s when St. Luke's Parish was established near the small community of Pritchardville. It was located south of the Broad River in what was then called Granville District (later to become Beaufort County). The Church (circa 1786) burned and was promptly rebuilt a short distance away in 1824. However, the original cemetery known as "the old burying ground" continued to be used, and that is where George was buried. My cousin Wes Cooler, III, and I have searched for the original site, but we have not located it. It appears to have vanished with the passing of many years and the advent of much modern development in the area.

The current structure (eventually sold to the United Methodists) still stands today on S.C. Highway 170. It is near the Charleston-Savannah Trail roadway — an extension of the King's Highway, a historic wagon trail covering more than 1,300 miles from Boston to the Savannah River. Many of my Cooler and some of my Harvey relatives are buried there.

Chapter 27

Growing Up With Jim Crow

I grew up in the 1950s in Coosawhatchie. My father's employment as a Manager for Stuckey's Stores later took me to numerous South Carolina and Florida locations. In 1961, Stuckey's built a store in Coosawhatchie, and I was able to return to where my life began. Like my mother Verna Wall and my sister Frances Harvey, I completed four years at Ridgeland High School. One thing remained unchanged. The Jim Crow era was still very much alive in the deep South.

During the early 20th century, my maternal Grandfather Lester Wall and numerous other prominent white male citizens of my South Carolina Lowcountry were members of the Ku Klux Klan. My mother told me the Klan marched in the holiday parades in Ridgeland. She said they all wore hoods, but she could always find her father by looking for his shoes.

In 1953, my father lost his job as a foreman helping build what we referred to as the "bomb plant" in New Ellington. Today, it is known as the Savannah River Plant. My parents and I returned to Coosawhatchie, where we lived in my Grandfather's small farm cabin at Bees Creek. We had no indoor plumbing, and we had one fireplace for heat. We used a small insulated "icebox" to keep milk cool. My father would drive to the icehouse in Ridgeland and buy one block of ice at a time. We used an artesian well for showers. My Grandfather built a wood enclosure around the well and connected a pipe with a showerhead. Taking a cold shower was not a choice. It was a necessity.

I was six years old, and I did not know we were poor. I just knew my parents loved me, and I enjoyed life on the farm. I helped take care of my Grandfather's Herford cows, pigs, and chickens. My grandparents lived in a large house in Coosawhatchie, and I knew my grandmother would always provide help when we needed it.

Our only neighbor was a black family who lived next door. They had a son my age, and he and I became friends. We played together every day, and we rode their mule together. His parents would share vegetables from their garden with us, and we would share seafood we caught from the Coosawhatchie River.

My mother would occasionally take me to Savannah, Georgia. Those were special trips. We would eat lunch in Morrison's Cafeteria and shop in the Sears Roebuck Department Store. On one of those visits to Sears, I went to the water fountain. My mother grabbed my arm and jerked me away as I was drinking. She whispered in my ear that I was drinking from the wrong fountain. She explained it was for the "colored" people. As soon as we got back home, I was on the mule with my friend. We couldn't go to school together; we couldn't drink from the same water fountain or use the same restroom. But we could play together until dark. I also noticed I never got sick drinking out of the same water dipper.

Growing Up With Jim Crow

My life on that small farm with no modern conveniences did not last long. Dad obtained an excellent job as the new Horne's store manager in Pocotaligo. The store had attached family quarters, and we enjoyed much-improved living conditions. I do not regret one minute living on that little farm. I learned life lessons there that I have never forgotten. One of those lessons was not to judge people by the color of their skin or their living conditions. Character is what matters.

In the early 1960s, while riding my bike one evening in Coosawhatchie, I came upon a Klan rally. The tall white cross was on fire, and a loudspeaker played a song. The only lyrics were "Run those (the N-word) North." This took place on U.S. Highway 17, one of the main routes from the Northeast to Florida. Very few cars were equipped with air conditioners, so most everyone traveled with their windows down in the summer. I now realize the "song" was for the benefit of the "Yankees" driving South and the black families who lived next door.

A Mule with Many Names.

https://www.trivalleylifechurch.org/wpcontent/uploads/2015/05/7395bca-21c855a7af34b75a9194b9efc.jpg. Retrieved December 12, 2021.

The Civil War In My South

My Grandmother Ethel Wall, Lester's wife, employed a black man to maintain her yard and plow her garden. His name was David. David referred to me as "Mr. Jimmy." I called him "David." I was 10. He was probably 70 years old at that time. I never knew his last name. Grandmother Ethel let David eat lunch in the kitchen instead of on the back porch, as was customary. She also drove him to Ridgeland when he needed to see a doctor. Lester didn't like any of this, but she persisted. I learned a lot from her that shaped my life from a young age.

My grandfather Lester Miles Wall's service station/motor court in Coosawhatchie, South Carolina. He is seen standing between the two children. The building was next to the Coosawhatchie River bridge on South Carolina's first State Highway 1.
1929

In the 1920s, Grandfather Lester built a combination service station/tourist court/diner on the Coosawhatchie River on U.S. Highway 17. The building had three restrooms for: "Men," "Women," and "Colored." As a teenager in the early 1960s, I worked there after school pumping gas and cleaning up the place. I was always told to keep the restrooms clean. I knew which restrooms I was to clean, but I decided to clean all three of them the same way. That was the first time I made a conscious decision to treat everyone with respect.

My mother, Verna Wall Harvey, on the left, and her Aunt Allene Belger Cooler. Allene was not much older, and they were best friends. They were standing under the first South Carolina State Highway sign on SC 1.This picture was taken next to the Coosawhatchie River Bridge in Coosawhatchie. circa 1928.

I am a proud native of South Carolina's Lowcountry. I love my state, and I always will. I also love America's history. It should be preserved, taught honestly and accurately, and include the bad with the good.

I cannot fully understand what it is like to be black in America. But, I continue to listen and try to understand. I supported the peaceful intent of those who marched in the protests during the summer of 2020. Let me be clear. I support "Black Lives Matter," the statement.

I do not support the Black Lives Matter Foundation, Inc. On July 13, 2013, this group was founded by three radical, Marxist women. I certainly do not support their plan to destroy the America I love.

This Foundation has done all it can to hijack those who do not support their agenda. Far-right and far-left radicals, including criminal thugs, invaded the protests with one goal: create violence, destroy historical monuments, steal as much property as they could, and start another civil war in America. Some large corporations and billionaires have failed to make this distinction (as well as most of our national media), either unknowingly or intentionally. They continue to donate millions of dollars to this radical organization and its supporters.

I am a retired law enforcement officer with 30 years of service in South Carolina. I believe most of those who participated in what they expected to be peaceful protests in 2020 used the statement "black lives matter" related to the unlawful killing of black men, women, and children by white police officers and white civilians. Had I been physically able, I would have marched with them.

Too many people hear "Black Lives Matter," the statement, and they assume it is the Black Lives Matter Foundation, Inc. They see peaceful protestors holding Black Lives Matter signs and believe they are part of the violent mob. Not all of them are.

However, the current movement rightly involves more than murdering innocent black people. It is also about affording all of the rights included in the U.S. Constitution to all of our citizens. And, it must also have an honest ongoing effort by white America to achieve genuine racial reconciliation with our black brothers and sisters.

Many white people are listening now, including those in positions of power in government, the entertainment industry, and corporate America. I earnestly hope the actions taken will result in real and lasting change for the benefit of everyone. I have never honored or supported racism in any form. And, I lament the actions of those who have and still do.

I do not, however, support the removal of statues, changing the names on buildings and commercial products, etc., that is now taking place. One might erase history, but one cannot change it.

I know this is important to many people. Will it lead to the lasting change we need? I don't think so. Until then, we must do all we can to right the wrongs for everyone as we find them.

I do support the creation of more monuments and other means of recognizing African Americans, Native Americans, and other minorities for their contributions to America.

To achieve lasting racial and ethnic reconciliation in our great nation, we must address our problems at their root cause. That cause is sin. This requires a change in the hearts of all of us. That change will only occur through true faith and repentance in Jesus Christ.

"History, despite its wrenching pain, cannot be unlived, but if faced with courage, need not be lived again."

Maya Angelou

Chapter 28

Conclusion

My research on the Civil War has led me to reach two conclusions.

If Abraham Lincoln and Jefferson Davis had reached out to one another and discussed a possible compromise to the crisis, the war might have been avoided. But, neither would make the first gesture to prevent what would be America's bloodiest conflict in history.

Second. I believe Robert E. Lee knew when he was offered and subsequently refused command of the United States Army that the Confederacy was already destined for defeat. While it was honorable for him to refuse to take up arms against his state and later assume command of the Army of Northern Virginia, he must have known the South's decision to secede from the Union would result in "the lost cause." The North had too many soldiers and too much industrial might to fail.

The Union's victory, won at a high cost of human suffering and death on both sides, was not unexpected. What was surprising was that it took four years to achieve. Had it not been for General Lee and his exceptional senior general staff, I think it would have been over much sooner. Lee gave his very best to avoid a Confederate defeat. After his surrender, he received much admiration from the South and the North for his character, leadership, and devotion to duty.

I also remain proud of my ancestors. During their service in the Confederate States Army, two were severely wounded. They stayed and performed non-combat duties. Three others were killed in action. All of them served with honor.

As previously indicated, my father, James Leslie Harvey, Sr., told me the story of my great grandfather's murder in the early 1950s when I was a young boy. But, it was not until the early 2000s that I began my research to determine and document the facts.

I encourage young people to ask their parents and grandparents, while they are still alive, to tell them their family history. If they wait like I did, no one will be alive to tell them.

On a personal note, I am pleased that my Great Grandfather was liked and respected by white and black citizens of South Carolina's Lowcountry. I am also pleased that my Grandfather Milledge Harvey and my Harvey-Cooler Great Uncles stood for justice instead of retribution. Their character and determination to uphold the law were not the norms during the Jim Crow years.

I remain disappointed that I have been unable to locate the Old Bull Hill Cemetery site in the Pritchardville area. Even if the site was found, I still could not determine where my Great Grandparents George and Eleanor Harvey were buried. I am also disappointed that the St. Luke's Church did not maintain the cemetery after they moved Mr. Bull's daughter's mausoleum to the front yard of the current church. The graveyard might not have been bulldozed over for modern development had they done so.

I am equally sad that the members of the First Baptist Church at Coosawhatchie did not maintain their cemetery following the Civil War. Today, only a few graves have visible markers remaining. This Colonial Cemetery is located on private property and is not accessible by the public.

Cemeteries are not pleasant places to visit, but they are essential to our lives. As Richard Lewellyn said in *How Green Was My Valley*, that is where we go to see those who have gone before us and to think of those who will come after us. That is where our family members are buried.

> *I saw behind me those who had gone, and before me, those who are to come. I looked back and saw my father, and his father, and all our fathers, and in front, to see my son, and his son, and the sons upon sons beyond. And their eyes were my eyes.*
>
> *As I felt, so they had felt, and were to feel, as then, so now, as tomorrow and forever. Then I was not afraid, for I was in a long line that had no beginning, and no end, and the hand of his father grasped my father's hand, and his hand was in mine, and my unborn son took my right hand, and all, up and down the line that stretched from Time That Was, to Time That Is, and is not yet, raised their hands to show the link, and we found that we were one, born of Woman, Son of Man, had in the Image, fashioned in the Womb by the Will of God, the Eternal Father.*

I was of them, they were of me, and in me, and I in all of them. [1]

Finally, I am most distressed about the divisiveness among America's citizens today. During my 75 years, I have never seen what we are experiencing now.

When Ronald Reagan was first elected as president of the United States, he asked U.S. Senator Strom Thurmond, from South Carolina, for advice on getting his legislative plan approved by Congress. Thurmond told him he would have to be willing to compromise. Reagan said he would not do that. Thurmond responded, "Well, Mr. President, you will not get anything done for this great country."

Failure to compromise brought us the Civil War. What will it get us today?

However, my hope is not found in governments, politicians, political parties, and special interest groups. My hope is found in my Savior, Jesus Christ. He is the King of Kings, and He is still on His throne. I will wait for Him.

But they who wait for the Lord
shall renew their strength;
they shall mount up with wings like eagles;
they shall run and not be weary;
they shall walk and not faint.

Isaiah 40:31 (ESV)

Grace and Peace to all.

End Notes

Preface

1. *Daily National Intelligencer,* Friday, July 27, 1832, Washington, DC., Issue: 6074, 3.

2. *South Carolina Declaration of Causes of Secession. December 24, 1860.* http://www.humanitiestexas.org/sites/default/files.pageattachment/Feller_Efforts%20to%20Compromise.pdf. Retrieved October 7, 2021.

3. Walter Donald Kennedy. *Myths of American Slavery.* Pelican Publishing Co. January 31, 2003.

Introduction

1. *Beaufort Gazette* newspaper. Beaufort, South Carolina. August 30, 1906. Retrieved from the Walker Local and Family History Center. Richland County Library, 1431 Assembly Street, Columbia, South Carolina.

2. *Yemassee Indians-Native Americans in S.C.* South Carolina Information Highway. https://www.sciway.net/hist/indians/yemassee.html. Retrieved February 10, 2020.

3. Lawrence S. Roland. *The History of Beaufort County, South Carolina.* Volume One. University of South Carolina Press. Columbia, SC. 1996 244.

4. J. D. Lewis. "The American Revolution in South Carolina," retrieved April 16, 2021. www.carolana.com/SC/Revolution.

5. James L. Harvey, Jr. *Coosawhatchie Baptist Church.* 1759 to 1861 & 1941 to 2020 (Lexington, South Carolina. 2021), 5.

6. Harvey, Coosawhatchie, 5.

7. Grace Fox Perry. *The Moving Finger of Jasper.* Churches. Golden Jubilee Edition. Jasper County Confederate Centennial Commission. 1962.

8. Perry, Churches

9. Perry, People.

Chapter 1

1. "United States Census, 1850, Family Search," NARA microfilm publication, Washington, D.C.: National Archives and Records Administration, n.d., accessed December 23, 2020, http://www.familysearch.org/ark:/61903/1:1:M8QK-31D.

2. Ellen Bush Jenkins and Posey Belcher. "Barnwell," South Carolina Encyclopedia, University of South Carolina, Institute for Southern Studies, August 19, 2021, https://www.scencyclopedia.org/sce/entries/barnwell/.

Chapter 2

1. Patricia Sabin. "Walterboro, South Carolina." SCGen Web-Colleton County, retrieved December 9, 2021. http://www.oldplaces.org/colleton/walterboro.html.

2. Lynzsg, "All in the Family Tree," Ancestry.com, March 20, 2020, https://www.ancestry.com/mediauiviewer/collection/1030/tree/7166601/person/232181765142/media/94b6f978-6799-4bee-b0af-87797385b85a?_phsrc=whx2714&usePUBJs=true

3. "Encyclopedia of the New American Nation," *Encyclopedia.com.* November 25, 2021, https://www.encyclopedia.com/history/encyclopedias-almanacs-transcripts-and-maps/overseers

Chapter 3

1. Jeff Fulgham, "The Bluffton Expedition: The Burning of Bluffton, South Carolina, During the Civil War." Lulu.com. July 10, 2013.

2. "Bluffton, South Carolina Population 2021 (Demographics, Maps, Graphs)" *World Population Review,* retrieved January 2, 2022, https://worldpopulationreview.com/us-cities/bluffton-sc-population.

3. Barry Kaufman. "Bluffton, SC: Where the Southern Secession Movement Took Root," *South Magazine*, February 8, 2017, http://www.southmag.com/bluffton-sc-where-the-southern-secession-movement-took-root/.

Chapter 4

1. "Flags of the Civil War-Southern Regimental and Unit Flags, *Historical Flags of Our Ancestors,* retrieved July 11, 2021, http://www.loeser.us/flags/civil-southern.html#top.

2. "Compiled Service Records of Confederate Soldiers Who Served in Organizations from the State of South Carolina," *The National Archives.* Carded Records Showing Military Service of Soldiers Who Fought in Confederate Organizations, compiled 1903 - 1927, documenting the period 1861 – 1865. Record Group 109. South Carolina. Roll: 0018.

3. Stewart Sifakis. *Compendium of the Confederate Armies.* Volume 7. South Carolina and Georgia. New York: Facts on File. 1992.

4. John C. Rigdon. "Historical Sketch And Roster Of The South Carolina 3rd Cavalry Regiment." *Eastern Digital Resources,* 2018.175.

Chapter 5

1. *War of the Rebellion: Serial 020 Page 0155 Chapter XXVI. SKIRMISH AT COOSAWHATCHIE, S.C., ETC. Numbers 5. Reports of Colonel Edward W. Serrell, First New York Engineers.* The Ohio State University College of Arts and Sciences. Center for Historical Research. Department of History. Dulles Hall, Room 106, 230 Annie & John Glen Ave., Columbus, OH.

Chapter 6

1. "Welcome to The Citadel," Information, retrieved September 15, 2021, http://www.citadel.edu/root/info.

End Notes

2. "Letter from Col. John C. Sellers," The Citadel Archives and Museum, retrieved September 15, 2021, http://www.citadeldigitalarchives.omeka.net/items/show/830.

Chapter 7

1. James M. Nichols. "48th New York Infantry: Perry's Saints, Or the Fighting Parsons Regiment in the War of Rebellion," AncestorStuff.com. retrieved May 10, 2021, https://www.ancestorstuff.com/new-york-perry-s-saints-or-the-fighting-parson-s-regiment-in-the-war-of-the-rebellion.-hardcover-49th-new-york-infantry.html.

2. "General order of General Beauregard. C.S. Army. General Orders NO 46," Headquarters Department of SC, GA, and FL, retrieved July 13, 2021, https://www.battleofpocotaligo.com/history.html.

Chapter 8

1. *Battle of Honey Hill*. https://www.wikiwand.com/en/Battle_of_Honey_Hil. Wikipedia. Retrieved September 16, 2021.

2. Charles Colcock Jones, *The Seige of Savannah*. Albany, NY. Joel Munsell. 1874.

3. John C. Rigdon. *Historical Sketch And Roster Of The South Carolina 3rd Cavalry Regiment*. (Cartersville, Georgia: Eastern Digital Resources, 2018), 39-40.

4. Matt Wallace, *Bittersweet: Black Virginians in Blue at the Battle of Honey Hill and Beyond. The* John L. Nav, III Center for Civil War History. University of Virginia. Charlottesville, Virginia. 2018.

http://naucenter.as.virginia.edu/blog-page/936. Retrieved March 26, 2022.

5. *The Confederate Account of the Battle of Honey Hill. Savannah Republican* newspaper. December 3, 1864.

6. Major General John G. Foster and Brigadier General John P. Hatch. *The War of the Rebellion: Official Records of the Civil War.* War of the Rebellion: Serial 065. Page 0002. S.C., Fla., and on the Ga. Coast. Chapter XLVII. The Ohio State University. Center for Historical Research. https://ehistory.osu.edu/books/official-records/065/0002. Retrieved August 16, 2021.

Chapter 9

1. Ronnie W. Faulkner. "Battle of Bentonville," Encyclopedia of North Carolina. http://*www.uncpress.org.* Retrieved December 6, 2021.

Chapter 10

1. Billy Moncure. "Overlooked and Overskilled: Rebel General Hampton," March 27, 2019. *Warhistroryonline.com/instant-articles/Hampton-legendary-legion-html.*

2. Ron Crawley. *A Chronological History of the Hampton Legion Battalion of Cavalry.* http://www.schistory.net/ironscouts/articles/hlcav.htm. 2001. Retrieved March 12, 2021.

3. *New York Times.* June 27, 1897. *https://www.newspapers.com/image/20340460/?terms=preston%20Hampton&match=1* Retrieved October 16, 2021.

4. Ibid. Crawley.

Chapter 11

1. E. Prioleau Henderson, *Autobiography of Arab* (Columbia, S.C.: The R. L. Bryan Company, 1901), 34.

Chapter 12

1. Steve A. Hawks. "Confederate Armies and Departments in the Eastern Theater. 11th Regiment, South Carolina Infantry," retrieved September 18, 2021, https://civilwarintheeast.com.

Chapter 13

1. "Report of Uzziah Rentz's Officer Medical Examining Board," Ancestry.com, retrieved May 16, 2015, https://www.ancestry.com/mediauiviewer/collection/1030/tree/70230248/person/46215438151/media/23cec815-a335-4c83-a496-a1e9c29b3e80?_phsrc=whx2839&usePUBJs=true.

2. DeWitt Boyd Stone, Jr., Editor. *Wandering To Glory* (Columbia, SC. University of South Carolina Press. 2002), 54.

3. Steve A. Hawks. *Confederate Armies and Departments in the Eastern Theater. 17th Regiment, South Carolina Infantry.* Retrieved September 18, 2021. https://civilwarintheeast.com.

4. "Historical Data Systems, comp. U.S. Civil War Soldier Records and Profiles," *1961-1965.* Ancestry.com Operations Inc. Provo, UT, U.S.A.

Chapter 14

1. "1850 United States Federal Census. Prince Williams Parish, South Carolina; Roll: M432_849; Page: 16A; Image: 338," Acestry.com, 2009.

2. *1850 United States Federal Census, 16A.*

3. *1860 United States Federal Census. St. Lukes Parish, Beaufort, South Carolina*; Roll: M653_1214; Page: 34; Image: 72; Family History Library Film: 805214.

4. "U.S. Civil War Soldiers, 1861-1865," Ancestry.com, Operations, Inc., 2007.

5. *1870 United States Federal Census. St. Luke's, Beaufort, South Carolina*; Roll: M593_1485; Page: 122B; Image: 248; Family History Library Film: 552984.

6. "1880 United States Federal Census, Coosawhatchie, Hampton, South Carolina," Ancestry.com and The Church of Jesus Christ of Latter-day Saints, 2010.

Chapter 15

1. Karen Stokes. *South Carolina Civilians In Sherman's Path. Stories of Courage Amid Civil War Destruction.*,(Charleston, SC: The History Press, 2012), 11.

2. "The Official Records of the Union and Confederate Armies." *War of Rebellion* (Washington, D.C.: Government Printing Office, 1880-1902).

End Notes

3. George W. Nichols, *The Story of the Great March, From the Diary of a Staff Officer* (New York: Harper & Brothers, 1865).

4. William Gilmore Simms, *Sack and Destruction of the City of Columbia, S.C.* (Columbia, S.C.: Power Press of Daily Phoenix, 1865).

5. Oliver Otis Howard, *Autobiography of Oliver Otis Howard* (New York: Baker & Taylor Company, 1907).

6. Simms. *Sack and Destruction*.

7. Michael Fellman, *Citizen Sherman: A Life of William Tecumseh Sherman (Modern War Studies)* Random House, 1995), 260-261.

8. Thomas G. Robisch. "General William T. Sherman: Would the Georgia Campaigns of the First Commander of the Modern Era Comply with Current Law of War Standards?" *Emory International Law Review 9*, No. 459, 1995, 461.

9. "William T. Sherman Correspondence," Villanova University Digital Library, Falvey Memorial Library. Retrieved March 26, 2022. https://digital.library.villanova.edu/Item/vudl:647248.

10. Jacqueline Glass Campbell, *When Sherman Marched North from the Sea. Resistance on the Confederate Home Front* (Chapel Hill: University of North Carolina Press. 2003).

11. Thomas Osborn. *Chicago to Appomattox: The 39th Illinois Infantry in the Civil War.* (McFarland & Company, Jefferson, North Carolina, 2021.) 153.

Chapter 16

1. William A. Courtenay, "Charles Jones Colcock," *Southern Historical Papers: Volume 26, 1898, 11.*

2. Courtenay, *Southern Historical,* 13-14.

Chapter 17

1. Earl Starbuck, *Robert E. Lee: The Soldier.* Abbeville Institute Press, May 5, 2021. Retrieved March 26, 2022. https://www.abbevilleinstitute.org/robert-e-lee-the--soldier/.

2. Daniel J. Crooks, Jr. *LEE IN THE LOWCOUNTRY.* (Charleston, SC: The History Press, 2008), 11.

3. John William Jones. *Personal Reminiscences, Anecdotes, and Letters of Gen. Robert E. Lee.* (New York. D. Appleton and Company, 1875) 13.

4. Clifford Dowdey and Louis H. Manarin, Editors. *The Wartime Papers of Robert E. Lee.* (New York: Da Capo Press, Inc., 1961), 97.

5. Crooks, *LEE IN THE LOWCOUNTRY,* 11-12.

Chapter 18

1. "General R. E. Lee's War-Horses, Traveller And Lucy Long." *Southern Historical Society Papers*, Vol. XVIII. January-December, 1890, https://www.civilwarhome.com/leeshorses.html.

Chapter 19

1. Captain Robert E. Lee, Jr., *Recollections and Letters of General Robert E. Lee.* Doubleday, Page & Company, New York, October 1904. Chapter 3. Pages 54-66.

Chapter 20

1. "1st South Carolina Volunteer Infantry Regiment (Colored)," Wikiwand, retrieved August 26, 2021,https://www.wikiwand.com/en/1stSouth_Carolina_Volunteer_Infantry_Regiment_(Colored)?wprov=srpw1_0. Wikipedia.

Chapter 21

1. "GN. FOSTER'S OPERATIONS. CAPTURE OF POCOTALIGO BRIDGE. The Savannah and Charleston Railroad Cut. SAVANNAH COMPLETELY ISOLATED. Foster's Scouts Said to be in Communication with Sherman. THE EXCHANGE OF PRISONERS, *New York Times,* December 13, 1864, 1.

Chapter 22

1. Douglas Southall Freeman. *R. E. Lee: A Biography, Pulitzer Prize Edition (4 Volume Set),* Charles Scribner's Sons. New York, 1934.

2. Tamela Baker, "Gen. Lee's Last Attempt to Avoid Surrender," *America's Civil War Magazine*, March 2015. 26-33.

Chapter 23

1. John C. Rigdon. *Historical Sketch And Roster Of The South Carolina 3rd Cavalry Regiment.* (Cartersville, Georgia: Eastern Digital Resources, 2018), 55-61.

Chapter 24

1. Gardiner H. Shattuck, Jr., *A Shield and Hiding Place: The Religious Life of the Civil War Armies.* Mercer University Press, Macon, Georgia, 1987.

2. Jeffery Warren Scott, with Mary Ann Jeffreys, "Fighters Of Faith," *Christian History* Magazine, Issue 33, 28-31.

3. "Christianity & the Civil War," *Christian History Magazine*, Issue 33, Inside Front Cover.

Chapter 25

1. "Eleanor Harvey Obituary." *The State,* March 21, 1902, 2.

2. "An Aged Citizen Brutally Killed," *The State,* August 28, 1906, 1.

3. "Murder Most Foul," *Palmetto Post,* August 30, 1906, 3.

4. "Negroes Gave Aid In Finding Criminal," *The State,* September 3, 1906. 1.

Chapter 26

1. *Beaufort Gazette,* September 23, 1906.

End Notes

Chapter 27

1. "A Mule with Many Names," Retrieved December 12, 2021, Life Church, https://www.trivalleylifechurch.org/2015/05/15/a_mule_with_many_names/. Posted May 15, 2015, by Loren.

Chapter 28

1. Richard Lewellyn, *How Green Was My Valley* (London: Penguin Books, 1939.

CPSIA information can be obtained
at www.ICGtesting.com
Printed in the USA
BVHW060758310522
638499BV00021B/438

9 781662 847745